**PICT**

C000040151

Santa Fe & Taos
plus the Enchanted Circle

Richard Harris

photographed by
Ellen and Hank Barone

Ulysses Press

Published by: Ulysses Press
P.O. Box 3440
Berkeley, CA 94703
www.ulyssespress.com

ISBN 1-56975-482-9

Printed in Canada by Transcontinental Printing

10 9 8 7 6 5 4 3 2 1

Interior photo credits: © Ellen and Hank Barone except for credits indicated on page 229
Cover photographs: All cover photos © Ellen and Hank Barone except front cover food image, which is courtesy of the New Mexico Department of Tourism (Dan Monaghan)
Design: Sarah Levin, Leslie Henriques
Editorial and production: Lynette Ubois, Claire Chun, Steven Schwartz, Lily Chou, Matt Orendorff, Tamara Kowalski
Indexer: Lily Chou
Maps: Pease Press

Distributed by Publishers Group West

Ulysses Press 🐢 is a federally registered trademark of BookPack, Inc.

PICTURE-PERFECT
escapes

Santa Fe & Taos
plus the Enchanted Circle

1.
Santa Fe and Beyond

Native cultures scoff at the notion that Christopher Columbus discovered this continent. Even as the Europeans trod through the Dark Ages, the Anasazi Indians were well into building intricate Chaco Canyon in northwestern New Mexico. In fact, the Pueblo Indians are thought to have come to Santa Fe around A.D. 1200 or 1300, and they were preceded for centuries by the Anasazi, well before Europeans ever dreamed of a New World.

The first Spanish settlers claimed this aptly named "Kingdom of New Mexico" in 1540 and the Spanish made Santa Fe a provincial capital in 1610. Over the next seven decades, Spanish soldiers and Franciscan missionaries sought to convert the Pueblo Indians of the region. Tribespeople numbered nearly

100,000, calling an estimated 70 burnt-orange adobe pueblos (or towns) home.

In 1680 the Pueblo Indians revolted, killing 400 of the 2500 Spanish colonists and driving the rest back to Mexico. The Pueblos sacked Santa Fe and burned most of the structures (save the Palace of the Governors), remaining in Santa Fe until Don Diego de Vargas reconquered the region 12 years later.

When Mexico gained independence from Spain in 1821, so too did New Mexico. Five years later, Santa Fe became an international trade center when the Santa Fe Trail was blazed from Missouri across the prairie to meet the Camino Real from Mexico City. But it wasn't until the Mexican-American War that an American flag flew over the territory. In 1848 Mexico ceded New Mexico to the United States and by 1912 New Mexico was a full-fledged state.

Why have people always flocked to this land of rugged beauty? The natural barriers surrounding sky-high Santa Fe, coupled with its obvious beauty, have always made it a desirable city and deserving capital, located at the crossroads of north and south.

Some maintain the lands around Santa Fe are sacred. Each year there's a pilgrimage to the modest Santuario de Chimayo church, said to be constructed on sacred and healing ground. American Indians, who successfully rejected the white man's attempts to force-feed them organized religion,

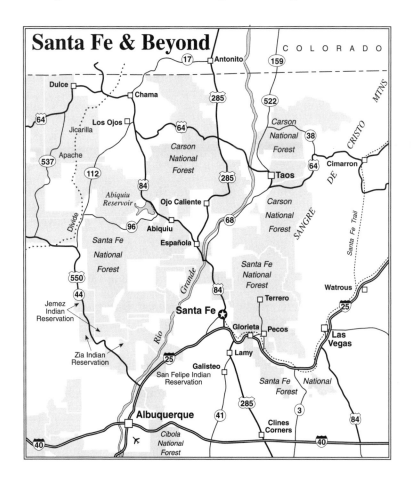

continue to have rituals and maintain sacred lands that remain secret to all outsiders.

Artist Georgia O'Keeffe brilliantly captured the magic light and intense colors around Santa Fe and Taos. The high-altitude sun creates shadows and vibrancies not to be believed, from subtle morning hues to bold and majestic evenings. Watching a sunset unfold over the Sangre de Cristo and Jemez mountains can be a spiritual experience as orange, pink and violet hues, chalk-colored pastels and lightning-bolt streaks of yellow overwhelm the sky. (Sangre de Cristo is Spanish for "Blood of Christ," a reference to the red hue that can color the mountains at sunset, especially when they are covered with snow.) Look around and you'll find bright splashes of color everywhere, such as the blood-red chile *ristras* lining highway stands framed against a big blue sky.

In fact, many of the area's earliest Anglo residents were painters, sculptors, musicians, novelists and poets. They came to Santa Fe and Taos for the same reason Gauguin went to Tahiti and Hemingway to Paris: to immerse themselves in exotic surroundings in hopes of finding new artistic dimensions. Today Santa Fe continues to grow as a regional arts center of international repute, boasting more than 200 art galleries, over 50 publishers, 16 performance stages and 14 major museums. Taos has a colorful history as an artists' and writers' colony, and continues as a thriving arts center in its own right.

Santa Fe Style Is Born

Many people who identify Santa Fe with its unique adobe-look architecture are surprised to learn that a hundred years ago it looked pretty much like any other Western town, with red brick Railroad Commercial buildings surrounding a New England-style town square and stately Victorian-style homes in the residential district.

Today's version of Santa Fe architecture dates back to 1909. Following the completion of a new territorial capital, the government planned to demolish the decrepit, 300-year-old Palace of the Governors, one of the last remaining adobe buildings in the downtown area. But the plan met with fierce opposition from an unlikely mix of archaeologists, architects, artists and old-timers. At the last minute, the palace was reprieved when the Archaeological Institute of America (now the School of American Research) agreed to take it over as their new headquarters and museum.

Archaeologists at the AIA proposed covering all the buildings surrounding the plaza with brown stucco to harmonize them with the palace, and although the project was never fully realized (some brick buildings were merely painted brown), the adobe-look fad soon swept through the city. Seeing it as a tourist draw, local boosters held a design contest for the new Fine Arts

Museum. Colorado architect Isaac Rapp won, basing his new Spanish Pueblo Revival building on old colonial mission churches on Indian pueblos.

Today, Rapp's style and the related Territorial Revival style (with red brick rooflines) are the only architectural styles allowed in the downtown historic district. However, very few adobe-look buildings in Santa Fe are actually made from adobe bricks, which are now very expensive.

Many Santa Fe and Taos residents, like the region's tourists, are here because of the climate. These high, dry mountain towns are pleasingly warm during spring and fall. Summer can bring intense heat and the winters are cold enough to make Santa Fe and Taos viable ski areas. Summer and fall are particularly popular among vacationers. Santa Fe averages 14 inches of rainfall a year, and 30 to 34 inches of snow.

The region's cultural mix is as colorful and varied as the weather. Anglo, Indian and Spanish peoples coexist, each group accepting of the others' beliefs yet holding strong to their own time-honored traditions. New generations living on the pueblos tend to follow popular culture and modern technology as much as their Anglo and Spanish neighbors do. Yet far from being homogenized by prosperity as has happened in other regions, the Pueblo Indians hold tight to their ancestral ceremonies and traditions, and most are fluent in one of the local Puebloan dialects—Tewa, Towa, Tiwa or Keres. The same goes for the physical remains in centuries-old Santa Fe. Rigorous zoning laws maintain Santa Fe's image by restricting architecture to either the Spanish Mission or Territorial Revival styles.

Tradition also blends well with modern culinary trends, as evidenced in the unusual local foods. While most area natives cultivate a taste for typical northern New Mexico dishes such as green chile stew and enchiladas, many restaurants also use local ingredients in original ways, giving rise to a unique fusion cuisine. It's not unusual to find such menu items as green chile polenta, blue corn crusted mahi mahi or piñon crème brulée.

For residents, Santa Fe life is not without its problems. Surrounded like an island by national forest, Indian land and waterless desert, the city can't keep up with real estate demand. Housing prices continue to skyrocket, making some longtime locals rich and banishing others to lower-rent digs in Española or Albuquerque. Fledgling artists find competition daunting in Santa Fe's high-priced galleries and typically live in outlying villages, selling their works in out-of-state exhibitions or on the arts-and-crafts-show circuit. And tensions run high between local residents chafing under extreme

water conservation regulations (in summer, outdoor water uses like washing your car or watering
your garden are usually completely banned) and golf
course developers who siphon off millions of gal-
lons of water daily. Meanwhile, lawyers engage in
endless battles over "dry water"—legal rights to
water that doesn't actually exist.

Rancho de las Golondrinas

On the whole, however, newcomers and long-
time residents alike agree that the quality of life
here can't be beat, and with a little planning and insight, visitors can experience for themselves what
makes Santa Fe so special. Avoiding summer holi-
day weekends, such as Memorial Day or Labor

Day—and especially local festivals such as Indian Market and Fiesta—means that favorite tourist spots will be less crowded and local Santa Feans more willing to have a chat. The city is quite beautiful in the fall, when the leaves are changing and the days are still balmy.

For a change of pace from the frontier sophistication of the capital city, take a trip out into the countryside, where you'll discover, in addition to boundless miles of desert and alpine wilderness, a scattering of unique towns and villages that often seem to be stranded in another time. South of Santa Fe is an old mining district where some historic settlements like Cerrillos and Madrid have risen from ghost town status to be born again as artists'

colonies, while others like Galisteo and Pecos cling to traditions that have endured since colonial times.

When you travel north, from Santa Fe to the much smaller tourist town of Taos 90 minutes away, the con-

All Aboard

Although the Atchison, Topeka and Santa Fe is one of the grand old names of the American rail system, Amtrak trains don't call on the capital city. Now, however, you can take the **Santa Fe Southern** south through scenic foothill country to the village of Lamy, the Amtrak stop closest to Santa Fe. In the summer, the tourist train leaves Monday, Tuesday, Thursday and Saturday; in winter, it runs Tuesday, Thursday and Saturday. Passengers can bring their own picnic lunches to dine on board or at Lamy. This excursion runs several hours ahead of the daily eastbound and westbound Amtrak trains. Admission. ~ Santa Fe Southern Railroad Depot, off Guadalupe Street, southwest of downtown; 505-989-8600, 888-989-8600, fax 505-983-7620; www.sfsr.com.

trast is even more striking. Along the Rio Grande you'll find a series of Indian pueblos, some of them dating back 800 years and now refurbished in the traditional manner with the proceeds of casino gambling. For the quintessential northern New Mexico experience, you can opt to follow the backroad route known as the High Road to Taos and discover little mountain villages such as Truchas and Las Trampas, where cattle graze in the dirt streets of town and the way of life seems not to have changed much since the 1700s. Along the way you can stop and see the famous Santuario de Chimayo, the holiest shrine in New Mexico.

Taos, which boasts the most picturesque of all the northern Indian pueblos right on the outskirts

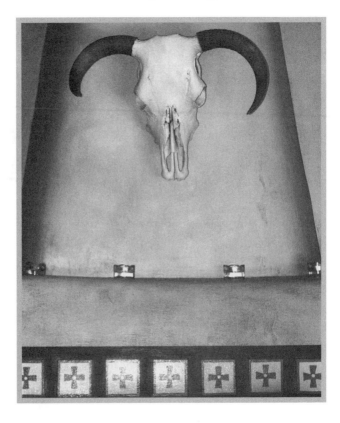

of town, is in some ways a junior version of Santa Fe. It has an abundance of art galleries—not hundreds of them, like Santa Fe, but enough so that you won't be able to browse through them all in a day. Taos is the only town in New Mexico that sees more visitors in winter than in summer since its ski area—on the slope of the highest mountain in the state—is as challenging as the legendary winter resorts across the state line in Colorado, and much less crowded.

PACKING AND PREPARATION

New Mexicans are casual in their dress and expect the same of visitors. Restaurants with dress codes are few and far between. Chic apparel in these parts is more likely to mean a western-cut suit, ostrich hide boots and a bolo tie with a flashy turquoise-and-silver slide, or for women, a fiesta dress with a concho belt, long-fringed moccasins and a squash blossom necklace—all fairly expensive items that you may never have an occasion to wear back home. Relax. Sporty, comfortable clothing will pass practically anywhere in Santa Fe and Taos.

When packing clothes, plan to dress in layers. Temperatures can turn hot or cold in a flash at any time of year. During the course of a single vacation day, you can expect to start wearing a heavy jacket, a sweater or flannel shirt and a pair of slacks or jeans, peeling down to a T-shirt and shorts as the day warms up, then putting the extra layers back on soon after the sun goes down.

Other essentials to pack or buy along the way include a good sunscreen and high-quality sunglasses. If you are planning to hike or even camp in the mountains during the summer, you'll be glad you brought mosquito repellent.

For outdoor activities, tough-soled hiking boots are more comfortable than running shoes on rocky terrain. Even noncampers may want to take along a backpacking tent and sleeping bag for irresistible urges to stay out under star-spangled New Mexico skies. A canteen, first-aid kit, flashlight and other routine camping gear may also come in handy. Cycling enthusiasts should bring their own bikes—there are a lot more great places to ride than there are places where you can find rentals. The same goes for golf and other activities that call for special equipment.

If you like to pick up free souvenirs—in the form of unusual stones, pine cones and the like—be sure to take along some plastic bags for hauling treasures. A camera, of course, is essential for capturing your travel experience; of equal importance is a good pair of binoculars, which let you explore distant landscapes from scenic overlooks. And don't, for heaven's sake, forget your copy of *Picture-Perfect Escapes Santa Fe & Taos*.

LODGING

Lodgings in the Santa Fe and Taos region run the gamut from tiny one-room mountain cabins to luxurious hotels that blend Indian pueblo architecture with contemporary elegance. Bed and breakfasts can be found not only in chic destinations like Santa Fe but also in such unlikely locales as former ghost towns and the outskirts of Indian reservations. They come in all types, sizes and price ranges. Typical of the genre are lovingly restored old mansions comfortably furnished with period decor, usually with under a dozen rooms. Some bed and breakfasts, however, are guest cottages or rooms in nice suburban homes, while others are larger establishments, approaching hotel size, of the type sometimes referred to as country inns.

The abundance of motels along Santa Fe's Cerrillos Road presents a range of choices, from name-brand motor inns to traditional mom-and-pop establishments that have endured since motels were invented.

At the other end of the price spectrum, the height of self-indulgent vacationing is to be found at upscale Santa Fe resorts, which offer riding stables, golf courses, tennis courts, fine dining, live entertainment and exclusive shops on the premises so that guests can spend their entire holidays without leaving the grounds—a boon for those seeking a few days' rest and relaxation, though such indulgence may mean missing out on experiencing the real New Mexico.

Other lodgings throughout the region offer a different kind of personality. Many towns—preserved historic

districts like Madrid and Cerrillos as well as larger communities like Taos—have historic hotels dating back before the turn of the century. Some of them have been lavishly restored to far surpass their original Victorian elegance. Others may lack the polished antique decor and sophisticated ambience but make up for it in their authentic feel.

Inn & Spa at Loretto

Whatever your preference and budget, you can probably find something to suit your taste with the help of

the regional chapters in this book. Remember, rooms can be scarce and prices may rise during the peak season, which is summer throughout most of the region and winter in Taos, New Mexico's premier ski town.

Accommodations in this book are organized by region and classified according to price. Rates referred to are high-season rates, so if you are looking for off-season bargains, it's good to inquire. *Budget* lodgings generally run less than $70 per night for two people and are satisfactory and clean but modest. *Moderate* hotels range from $70 to $110; what they have to offer in the way of luxury will depend on where they are located, but they generally offer larger guest rooms and more attractive surroundings. At *deluxe*-priced accommodations, you can expect to spend between $110 and $180 for a homey bed and breakfast or a double in a hotel or resort. In hotels of this price you'll generally find spacious rooms, a fashionable lobby, a restaurant and often a group of shops. *Ultra-deluxe* facilities, priced above $180, are a region's finest, offering all the amenities of a deluxe hotel plus plenty of extras.

Room rates vary as much with locale as with quality. Downtown Santa Fe, for instance, has no rooms at all in the budget price range. The price categories listed in this book are relative, designed to show you where to get the most out of your travel budget, however large or small it may be.

DINING

Restaurants seem to be one of the main industries in some parts of New Mexico. Santa Fe, for example, has approximately 300 restaurants—this in a city of under

Colorful Cuisine

New Mexico's distinctive cuisine has strong roots in the Pueblo Indian culture as adapted by Spanish settlers. It is set apart from Tex-Mex and Mexican food by three ingredients that are unique to the state.

Green chile, which is ubiquitous in New Mexican restaurants and kitchens, is the same hot pepper that is crushed into chili powder—in fact, New Mexico produces virtually all of the chili powder in the United States—but locals prefer to harvest it before it turns red and eat it as an ultra-spicy vegetable. Grown mainly in the small communities of Hatch and Chimayo, it is sold by the bushel during the late August to mid-September harvest season. The seller roasts the chiles, making the inedible outer skin easy to remove, and the buyer divides them into bags and freezes them to last the rest of the year. Green chile is almost never served outside New Mexico. If the plant is grown elsewhere, the green chile pods lose their flavor, as they do when dried or canned. Enjoy it while you can. If you want to take the taste of New Mexico home as a souvenir, your best bet is green chile preserves, sold in many Santa Fe and Taos curio shops.

Blue corn, a variety of Indian maize, has been cultivated by the Pueblo people for at least 1200 years. They hold it sacred because it is the color of the sky and of turquoise, the most precious of stones among Southwestern Indians. Spanish settlers grew blue corn obtained

100,000 people. While the specialty cuisine throughout most of New Mexico consists of variations on Mexican and Indian food, you'll find many restaurants catering to customers whose tastes don't include hot chile peppers. You'll also find a growing number of restaurants offering "New Southwestern" menus that feature offbeat dishes using local ingredients. Green-chile tempura? Snow-crab enchiladas? If a newly invented dish sounds tempting, by all means give it a try!

from the Indians, and it accounts for much of the corn grown in New Mexico today. The corn kernels have tough outer shells and so cannot be eaten directly off the cob. Instead, they are traditionally crushed into meal, mixed with water and made into tortillas or ground into a fine powder and boiled in water to make a souplike beverage called *atole*, which Indian shamans and Spanish *curanderos* claim has healing powers.

Piñon nuts form inside the cones of the piñon trees that dot the hills and mesas of northern New Mexico. All the trees in a particular area produce nuts at the same time, but only once every seven years. Local villagers harvest them by placing a sheet around the bottom of a tree, then lassoing the treetop with a rope and shaking it vigorously until the nuts fall out. The nuts are then sold by the roadside or whole-saled to local supermarkets. It is a common practice in northern New Mexico to mix piñon nuts, shell and all, with whole-bean coffee and grind them together, giving the coffee a rich, chocolatelike flavor. Coffee with piñon is sold in many supermarkets and makes an unusual souvenir or gift.

Within a particular chapter, restaurants are categorized by region, with each entry describing the establishment according to price. All serve lunch and dinner unless otherwise noted. Surprisingly, stiff competition means that restaurant prices—especially outside the downtown area—tend to run somewhat lower than at comparable establishments in other cities. Dinner entrées at *budget* restaurants usually cost $8 or less. The ambience is in-formal, service usually speedy and the crowd often a local one. *Moderately* priced restaurants range between $8 and $16 at dinner; surroundings are casual but pleasant, the menu offers more variety and the pace is usually slower. *Deluxe* establishments tab their entrées from $16 to $24; cuisines may be simple or sophisticated, depending on the location, but the decor is plusher and the service more personalized. *Ultra-deluxe* dining rooms, where entrées begin at $24, are often the gourmet places; here cooking has become a fine art and the service should be impeccable.

Some restaurants change hands often and are occasionally closed in low seasons. Efforts have been made in this book to include places with established reputations for good eating. Breakfast and lunch menus vary less in price from restaurant to restaurant than evening dinners. All restaurants in this book serve lunch and dinner unless otherwise noted.

CALENDAR OF LOCAL EVENTS

JANUARY   More than two dozen local restaurants compete for the Best Soup in Santa Fe title in the charitable fundraiser **Souper Bowl Sunday**.

Most pueblos have **Transfer of Canes of Authority** ceremonies on New Year's Day and celebrate the new tribal officers with animal dances on **Three Kings Day**. San Ildefonso Pueblo's **Fiesta de San Ildefonso** features all-day animal dances, including an awe-inspiring dawn procession descending from Black Mesa. Picuris and San Juan pueblos observe the **Fiesta de San Pablo** with ceremonial dances.

In Taos, the **Winter Wine Festival** includes tastings and a silent auction to benefit the Nature Conservancy.

FEBRUARY The Santa Fe Gallery Association sponsors **The Edible Art Tour**, featuring elaborate *ouvres* by some of Santa Fe's top chefs. Later in the month, La Fonda Hotel offers food and wine tastings at its **Winefest**.

Picuris Pueblo celebrates **Candelaria** (Candlemas).

Participants "ski" the snow slopes with shovels at the annual **Shovel Races** in Angel Fire. At Taos Ski Valley, **Super Ski Week** presents workshops for intermediate and advanced skiers. It is followed by **Masters Ski Week** (for skiers over age 50) and **Telemark Ski Week**.

MARCH The **Southwest Snowboard Championships** are held at the Santa Fe Ski Basin.

Most pueblos hold dances on **Easter weekend**.

Taos Ski Valley holds two **Teen and College Ski Weeks**. The weekend-long **Ernie Blake Celebration** commemorates the ski valley's founder with a weekend of music, games, fireworks and a torchlight parade.

APRIL Beginning on the Thursday before Easter, thousands of faithful from all over New Mexico line the high-

PICTURE-PERFECT
Community Events

1. **Santa Fe Indian Market,** *p. 24*
2. **Fiestas de Santa Fe,** *p. 24*
3. **Traditional and Contemporary Spanish Markets,** *p. 23*
4. **Eight Northern Pueblos Arts and Crafts Fair,** *p. 24*
5. **Taos Pow-Wow,** *p. 24*

Fiestas de Santa Fe

Fiestas, the big community celebration that marks the end of Santa Fe's summer tourist season, takes place on the weekend following Labor Day, from Thursday evening through Sunday evening. The event began as a commemoration of the Spanish colonists' return to New Mexico after the Pueblo Revolt of 1680. It was religious in nature, though it was celebrated in midsummer rather than on the traditional October feast day of St. Francis, Santa Fe's patron saint. After New Mexico became United States Territory, the fiesta was moved to September so it would not clash with the Fourth of July.

"Fiesta" became "Fiestas" in 1883, when promoters of a territorial fair in Santa Fe decided to charge admission to the church processions. In protest, Santa Feans organized a free secular fiesta at the same time as the religious one. The new Fiestas de Santa Fe has been held annually except in wartime ever since. Fiestas features parades including a reenactment of the triumphant arrival of the Spaniards in Santa Fe, a tongue-in-cheek Historical-Hysterical Parade and a children-and-pets parade, as well as street dancing. The opening event, the burning of Zozobra (a 40-foot-tall, fireworks-filled puppet representing "Old Man Gloom") dates back to 1926, when it was invented by Will Schuster, one of Santa Fe's original artists.

ways from Santa Fe to Chimayo in the **Chimayo Pilgrimage**, the largest religious pilgrimage in the U.S.

The **Taos Picture Show**, the longest-established film festival in New Mexico, features films from around the world.

MAY Santa Feans observe **All Species Day** with a costumed parade and a festival in Fort Marcy Park. Later in the month, **CommUNITY Days** fills the plaza with revelers and displays by the City Different's nonprofit organizations.

Taos Pueblo holds its **Blessing of the Fields and Corn Dance**, complete with traditional foot races.

The **Taos Spring Arts Celebration**, continuing over several weekends, features artists' studio tours, performing arts and live entertainment.

JUNE The **Spring Festival and Animal Fair** at Rancho de las Golondrinas near Santa Fe presents Spanish Colonial craft demonstrations and re-creates 17th-century hacienda life. **The Santa Fe Opera** season opens with hundreds of tailgate parties and the city's accommodations fill to capacity through August.

Tesuque Pueblo holds its **Blessing of the Fields**. San Juan Pueblo observes the **Fiesta de San Juan** with buffalo and Comanche dances. San Ildefonso, Santa Clara, San Juan, Picuris and Taos pueblos have Comanche or corn dances on the **Fiesta de San Antonio**. Picuris Pueblo hosts its **High Country Arts and Crafts Festival**. The **Fiesta de San Juan** is the occasion for foot races and animal dances through the night and day at San Juan Pueblo.

The Taos School of Music **Summer Chamber Music Festival**, which runs through August, combines concerts by top classical musicians with educational seminars.

JULY The **Rodeo de Santa Fe** comes to the state capital with a parade. A **Fourth of July Pancake Breakfast** is held on the Plaza. The **Traditional and Contemporary Spanish Markets** fill the Plaza with works by 400 area artists and craftspersons. Rancho de las Golondrinas hosts the **New Mexico Wine Festival**.

Nambe Pueblo holds its **Waterfall Ceremonial** on the 4th of July. Taos Pueblo hosts its colorful annual **Taos Pow-Wow**. The **Eight Northern Pueblos Arts and Crafts Fair**, held each year at a different Indian pueblo north of Santa Fe, hosts hundreds of American Indian exhibitors. Taos Pueblo holds corn dances on the **Fiesta de Santiago** and the **Fiesta de Santa Ana**.

The **Taos Fiesta** fills the streets with a parade and music.

AUGUST   The largest non-ethnic **Arts and Crafts Fair** of the year is held on Santa Fe's Plaza the first weekend of August. The **Santa Fe County Fair** offers a look at the produce and livestock of nearby farms and ranches. The **Santa Fe Indian Market**, the largest American Indian arts show and sale anywhere, draws collectors from around the world on the third weekend of the month. The **Summer Festival and Frontier Market** at Rancho de las Golondrinas features an old-fashioned mountain-man gathering.

Santa Clara Pueblo has corn, buffalo and Comanche dances during the **Fiesta de Santa Clara**. A corn dance is held at Picuris Pueblo on **San Lorenzo Feast Day**.

Music from Angel Fire, held at the Village House, hosts national classical and jazz artists.

SEPTEMBER   The **Fiestas de Santa Fe** starts with the ritual burning in effigy of a 40-foot-tall "Old Man Gloom" and continues through a weekend of parades, processions and wild celebration. The **Barkin' Ball** benefit for the Santa Fe Animal Shelter includes cocktails, dinner and dancing; guests' dogs are welcome. The **Santa Fe Wine and Chile Fiesta** offers tastings of 200 wines and food from 70 restaurants.

San Ildefonso Pueblo has a corn dance on the **Fiesta de Navidad de Santa María**. Taos Pueblo celebrates the **Fiesta de San Geronimo** with buffalo, Comanche and corn dances, a trade fair, foot races and a pole climb.

The **Taos Arts Festival** which runs September to mid-October, presents art exhibits, lectures and a crafts fair.

OCTOBER　Costumed volunteers re-create the Spanish Colonial era at **Harvest Festival** at the Rancho de las Golondrinas, a historic hacienda located near Santa Fe. Many nearby villages hold **Artists' Studio Tours**.

A corn or elk dance marks the **Fiesta de San Francisco** at Nambe Pueblo.

NOVEMBER   The Santa Fe Ski Team sponsors a fundraising **Ski Swap**. The **Opening Day at Santa Fe Ski Basin** is normally on the day after Thanksgiving.

Tesuque Pueblo celebrates the **Fiesta de San Diego** with various dances.

DECEMBER   **Winter Spanish Market** entices Christmas shoppers with traditional arts and crafts. The **Santa Fe Film Festival** features premieres of new independent films. The Christmas holidays hold particular charm in

Santa Fe and Taos, where instead of colored lights, building exteriors glow with thousands of small candles called *farolitos*. **Las Posadas** re-creates Joseph and Mary's search for lodging. Thousands of Santa Feans take the Christmas Eve **Farolito Walk** up Canyon Road.

Pojoaque Pueblo holds dances in observance of the **Fiesta de Guadalupe**. Torchlight processions, vespers and *matachines* dances mark **New Year's Eve** at Taos, San Juan and Tesuque pueblos. **Christmas Day** is celebrated with more dances at Tesuque, San Ildefonso, Santa Clara, San Juan, Picuris and Taos pueblos;

the following day, San Juan Pueblo has a turtle dance. Children dance at Santa Clara and Picuris pueblos on **Holy Innocents' Day.**

OUTDOOR ACTIVITIES

Fishing

Use bait or fly, but don't head home without taking back some tall fish tales from your trip to the Santa Fe area. Pack your pole and perambulate over to the Pecos River or one of the region's lakes.

SANTA FE AREA   In the Santa Fe area, the fish are probably biting at the Pecos River. In the upper reaches of the canyon, all fishing is catch-and-release. If you want to eat the trout you catch, head for Monastery Lake, on the river just north of Pecos and downstream from the state trout hatchery. Try **High Desert Angler** for fishing tackle rental and flyfishing guide service. ~ 435 South Guadalupe Street; 505-988-7688. Bait is available at **Adelo's Town and Country Store** in Pecos. ~ 505-757-8565.

SANTA FE TO TAOS   **Nambe Lake**, on the Nambe Pueblo reservation, is well stocked with rainbow trout; a state fishing license is not required, but a day-use fee is charged.

TAOS AND THE ENCHANTED CIRCLE   Anglers find the fishing grand in these parts. Near Taos, head for the Rio Grande. Roads run to the river at Orilla Verde and Wild Rivers Recreation Areas. More adventuresome anglers can hike down the steep volcanic cliffs of the Rio Grande Gorge to remote stretches of the river in search of trophy-size rainbow and brown trout.

Los Rios Anglers sells and rents flyfishing tackle and guides half- and full-day fishing trips along the Rio

Grande and its tributaries. ~ 126 West Plaza Drive, Taos; 505-758-2798. In the summer, tackle is available at **Cottam's Skiing and Outdoor Shop**. ~ 207-A Paseo del Pueblo Sur; 505-758-2822; www.cottamsskishops.com. **Dos Amigos Anglers Co.** provides bait and tackle in Eagle Nest. They also offer instruction, half- as well as full-day flyfishing trips. ~ 247 Therma Drive; 505-377-6226.

River Running

Shooting the rapids is an increasingly popular activity in the Santa Fe area, and you can get your feet wet on a guided tour of the tumultuous Rio Grande or the tame Rio Chama. Both rivers have been designated by the United States government as Wild and Scenic Rivers, with environmental protection similar to federal wilderness areas. Both are full of river rafts and kayaks during the late spring and early summer. when the rivers are swollen with runoff from snow-melt in the nearby mountains. Weekend releases of water from El Vado Lake near Rio Chama keep the river flowing all summer long. Many outfitters are ready and willing to help immerse you in the fun of wave riding.

SANTA FE   Although the Santa Fe River rarely flows, several Santa Fe–based rafting companies shuttle the adventurous northward for tours. **New Wave Rafting Co.** runs daily tours from Santa Fe in rafting season, including overnight trips on the Rio Grande and three-day runs on Rio Chama. Food and gear are provided. ~ Route 5, Box 302-A; 505-984-1444, 800-984-1444; www.new waverafting.com. Another outfitter for the region is **Santa Fe Rafting**, which offers half-day, full-day, evening and overnight trips on the Rio Grande and the Chama. ~ 1000 Cerrillos Road; 505-988-4914, 800-467-7238; www. santaferafting.com. **Kokopelli Rafting Adventures** embarks on half- and full-day whitewater excursions on the Rio Grande and the Rio Chama (class II to class IV rapids). They also have inflatable kayak trips on the river and sea kayaks on some of the local lakes. Food is provided. ~ 551 West Cordova Road #540; 505-983-3734, 800-879-9035; www.kokopelliraft.com.

TAOS AND THE ENCHANTED CIRCLE West of Taos, the Rio Grande flows through a spectacular 400-foot-deep gorge nicknamed the Taos Box. There are several rafting guide services in the Taos area. **Los Rios River Runners** takes half-day, full-day and overnight trips on the Class I, III and V rapids of the Rio Grande—including the Taos Box—and the smooth current of the Rio Chama. If you really want to go all out, they'll arrange for an astronomer, a Celtic musician, a yoga teacher or a wine expert to accompany you. All meals, tents and camping gear are provided. ~ P.O. Box 2734, Taos, NM 87571; 505-776-8854, 800-544-1181; www.losriosriver runners.com, e-mail whitewater@newmex.com. **Native**

PICTURE-PERFECT
Adventures

Sons Adventures also guides whitewater raft trips through the Class II to IV Taos Box and the Class II and III Lower Gorge (a good starting trip for beginners). ~ 1033 Paseo del Pueblo Sur; 505-758-9342, 800-753-7559; www.nativesonsdventures.com. **Far Flung Adventures** operates out of El Prado and runs the Taos Box and the Rio Chama. They offer half-day, full-day and overnight trips. Meals and tents are provided. ~ P.O. Box 707, El Prado, NM 87529; 505-758-2628, 800-359-2627; www.farflung.com.

Swimming

Splash around in one of the several public pools in Santa Fe. Take a Santa Fe splash at the **Salvador Perez Pool**. ~ 601 Alta Vista Street; 505-955-2604. Also in the area is the the **Tino Griego Pool**. ~ 1730 Llano Street; 505-955-2661. The **Alto/Bicentennial Pool** opens in late May for summer swims. ~ 1121 Alto Street; 505-955-2650 (in summer). **Genoveva Chavez Community Center** has an Olympic-size pool and another outfitted with a water-slide. ~ 3221 Rodeo Road; 505-955-4001.

Skiing

Don't be fooled by the seemingly dry New Mexico land-scape: The mountains are situated in a moisture belt that in an average year receives more snow than the Colorado Rockies. When storm clouds part, be prepared for warm, sunny days in the high desert. The ski season runs from Thanksgiving through April, weather permitting, but may vary from resort to resort.

SANTA FE AREA　How many capital cities have a full-service ski area within a 30-minute drive? **Ski Santa Fe**, located up the winding, twisting Hyde Park/Ski Basin Road, 17 miles northeast of the Plaza, has six lifts and 45 trails—20 percent beginner, 40 percent intermediate and 40 percent advanced—covering 460 skiable acres with a vertical drop of 1703 feet. There are no limits on snow-boarding. Ski and snowboard rentals and lessons for chil-dren and adults are available. ~ Route 475; 505-982-4429, fax 505-986-0645; www.skisantafe.com, e-mail info@skisantafe.com.

The **Santa Fe Nordic Ski Area**, located just west of Ski Basin Road about two miles from the downhill ski slopes, is groomed by a local ski club to offer an array of cross-country ski challenges designed for racing practice but suitable for all skill levels. ~ Santa Fe National Forest, Vegas District; 505-425-3534.

TAOS AND THE ENCHANTED CIRCLE　This area boasts New Mexico's best alpine skiing. In fact, Taos Ski Area is so popular that Taos has become the only town in New Mexico where winter, not summer, is the peak tourist season. The ski season runs roughly from Thanksgiving through March, but may begin earlier or end later depending on weather conditions. Ski rentals and instruction are available at all the resorts listed here.

Granddaddy of New Mexico's alpine ski resorts is **Taos Ski Valley**, with a summit elevation of nearly 12,000 feet and a vertical drop of 2612 feet. Taos boasts more than 1000 acres of bowls and chutes served by ten chairs and two surface lifts. Taos has a reputation as one of the most challenging ski areas in the Rocky Mountains, with about half of the trails designated as expert. Snow conditions at Taos Ski Valley are available 24 hours a day by calling 505-776-2916. ~ Route 150/Taos Ski Valley Road; 505-776-2291; www.skitaos.org, e-mail tsv@skitaos.org.

Forty-five minutes away from Taos, **Red River Ski Area** is an increasingly popular family ski area with a 1600-foot vertical drop. Seven lifts serve 290 acres of trails, rated 32 percent beginner, 38 percent intermediate and 30 percent expert. Snowboarding is allowed. Snow

Airdog Alert

Sipapu Ski Area—the oldest ski slope in northern New Mexico, built in 1952—is especially popular with snowboarders thanks to its two terrain parks. The small ski area covers only 65 acres, with a peak elevation of just over 9000 feet and a 1055-foot vertical drop. Four lifts serve 31 trails: 20 percent beginner, 50 percent intermediate and 30 percent expert. ~ Route 518, Vadito; 505-587-2240, 800-587-2240; www.sipapunm.com, e-mail customer service@sipapunm.com.

conditions at Red River are available 24 hours a day by calling 505-754-2220. ~ Route 38, Red River; 505-754-2223; www.redriverskiarea.com, e-mail redriver@newmex.com. An even gentler ski area is **Angel Fire**, where five lifts carry skiers up to 10,677 feet elevation for a vertical descent of 2077 feet on 31 percent beginner, 48 percent intermediate and 21 percent expert trails. Snowboarding is allowed on all runs as well as in the terrain park. ~ Route 434; 505-377-6401, 800-633-7463.

Cross-country skiers who prefer the peaceful sounds of nature will enjoy gliding through the **Enchanted Forest**, which has no services save for a warming hut. ~ Route 38, Red River.

Ski Rentals   To rent your sticks in Taos, visit **Cottam's Skiing and Outdoor Shop**, where they will set you up with downhill and cross-country skis, snowboards and snowshoes. ~ 207-A Paseo del Pueblo Sur; 505-758-2822; www.cottamsskishops.com.

Angel Fire Resort Rental Shop at the mountain base rents snowboards, snowshoes, skis and downhill and Nordic equipment. They also offer repairs and tunings. ~ Angel Fire; 800-469-9327; www.angelfirenm.com. **SkiTech Discount Ski Rentals**, convenient to Angel Fire, rents downhill and cross-country skis, snowboards and snowblades. ~ North Angel Fire Road, Village Center; 505-377-3213, 800-531-7547. For cross-country ski or snowshoe rentals, lessons or a moonlight ski tour, check in at **Millers Crossing**, a shop that runs the ski area at Enchanted Forest. ~ 417 West Main Street, Red River; 505-754-2374, 800-966-9381; www.enchantedforestxc.com.

Golf

Believe it or not, the New Mexico desert harbors great golfing. Lush courses provide a cool respite from summer heat and primo playing conditions even in the dead of winter. (And there's no charge for the fabulous scenery.) Most courses have club and cart rentals as well as a resident pro.

SANTA FE   Practice your swing on the 18-hole semiprivate course or driving range at the **Santa Fe Country Club.** ～ 1000 Country Club Drive; 505-471-0601. The public **Marty Sanchez Links de Santa Fe** has both an 18-hole championship course and a par-3, 9-hole course offering mountain views. A driving range, putting green and pro shop are additional features. ～ 205 Caja del Rio; 505-955-4400.

SANTA FE TO TAOS   The public **Towa Golf Resort** at Pojoaque Pueblo has 27 holes, with nine more slated to open soon after this book goes to press. Any two of the par-36 nine-hole courses can be played together. ～ 17746 Route 84/285; 505-455-9000.

The **Black Mesa Golf Club**, set partly on Indian land and co-owned by Santa Clara Pueblo and private developers, is an 18-hole desert course with natural fairway vegetation, California greens and dramatic "badlands" surroundings. It was voted "Best New Affordable Public Golf Course for 2003" by *Golf Digest*. ～ 115 Route 399, La Mesilla; 505-747-8946; www.blackmesagolfclub.com.

Tennis

Santa Fe vacationers can take a swing at any of several municipal courts—**Atalaya Park** (717 Camino Cabra; two courts), the **Fort Marcy Complex** (Old Taos Highway and Morales Road; two courts) and **Larragoite Park** (Agua Fria Street and Avenida Cristobal Colon; two courts). All have hard-surface public courts for daylight use only, first-come, first-served. **Alto Park** (1121 Alto Street), **Herb Martínez/La Resolana Park** (2240 Camino

Carlos Rey) and **Salvador Pérez Park** (610 Alta Vista Street) have four lighted courts each. Court information is available at 505-955-2100.

Riding Stables

Wondering how to acquire that true Western swagger? Hop in the saddle and ride the range—or just take a lesson—with one of the several outfitters in the area.

SANTA FE AREA   For a unique riding experience, the **Broken Saddle Riding Company** offers one- to three-hour small group tours of the Cerrillos Hills, site of historic turquoise and silver mines, on well-trained Tennessee Walkers and Missouri Fox Trotters. ⁓ Cerrillos; 505-424-7774; www.brokensaddle.com.

You can saddle up at **Bishop's Lodge**, where daily guided trail rides follow Tesuque Creek into the Sangre de Cristo foothills. ⁓ Bishop's Lodge Road, Santa Fe; 505-983-6377, 800-732-2240; www.bishopslodge.com. **Vallecitos Stables** offers two- to five-hour guided trail

rides through mountain meadows and forests. ~ P.O. Box 1214, Vallecitos, NM 87581; 505-582-4221, 800-797-7261; www.vallecitosstables.com.

TAOS AND THE ENCHANTED CIRCLE   Beautiful terrain and varied trails make this a great area to see on horseback. Several ranches in the region run tours. Ride with American Indians on the Great Spirit's property at the **Taos Indian Horse Ranch**, where tribal guides lead groups of one to twenty riders on two-hour and longer tours through parts of Taos Pueblo's mountainous 100,000-acre reservation. Children's rides are also available. Reservations required. ~ 1 Miller Road, Taos Pueblo; phone/fax 505-758-3212.

East of Taos, one-hour to half-day trail rides are offered by **Roadrunner Tours, Ltd.** You can also take an overnight camping trip on horseback or join a cattle drive on the alpine 10,000-acre CS Ranch. ~ Route 434, Angel Fire; 505-377-6416, 800-377-6416.

Biking

If you haven't noticed the high altitude yet, why not get in touch with your surroundings by going for a two-wheeled spin? You'll be amply rewarded for your huffing and puffing with breathtaking views.

SANTA FE AREA   From the Santa Fe Plaza, pedal to Ski Basin Road, which takes cyclists up a windy and at times steep 17-mile two-lane road through heavily wooded national forest land to the **Ski Santa Fe** area. To enjoy a shorter trip at a more forgiving altitude (the ski area is at 10,400 feet), just ride the eight miles to **Hyde State Park**.

A killer ten-mile ride for mountain bikers starts north of the Picacho Hotel on St. Francis Drive, crosses Dead Man's Gulch and Camino La Tierra before heading into the foothills of **La Tierra**. Circle back to the hotel via Buckman Road.

The most spectacular mountain-bike trip in the Santa Fe area starts at **Aspen Vista**, on Ski Basin Road midway between Hyde Park and the ski area. A six-mile access road for the broadcast towers on top of 12,010-foot Tesuque Peak is off-limits to motor vehicles but open to cyclists. It offers a long climb through a shimmering aspen forest, ending with a panoramic view of the Pecos Wilderness from a perch at the edge of a sheer cliff that drops 2000 feet to inaccessible Santa

Fe Lake. Coasting back down is a mountain bikers' thrill of a lifetime.

TAOS AND THE ENCHANTED CIRCLE The scenic mountain roads are perfect for bicycle rides of all lengths and levels. A relatively difficult five-mile loop trail called **Devisadero** allows for a good view of the town of Taos. Start across from the El Nogal picnic area on Route 64 and get ready to climb 1300 vertical feet of elevation.

La Jara Canyon (Route 64, on the horseshoe between Taos and Angel Fire) is a meandering two-mile climb to an alpine meadow that appeals especially to those new in the (bike) saddle.

Wait until late afternoon to take the three-mile **Cebolla Mesa Trail** (Route 522, about 18 miles north of Taos) for the splendid sunsets. Pedal near the rim of the 800-foot Rio Grande Gorge at Cebolla Mesa. Start the trip at the intersection of Cebolla Mesa Road and Route 522 and ride to the campground.

Bike Rentals   In Santa Fe, **Sun Mountain Bike Rental**, located in El Centro, offers mountain-bike rentals, plus beginning to expert mountain-bike tours. Grab a latte from their espresso bar while suiting up. ~ 102 East Water Street; 505-982-8986; www.sunmountainbikeco.com. **Gearing Up Bicycle Shop** rents mountain bikes, sells new bicycles and accessories and has a repair shop on the premises. Shuttle services are also available to trails around the area. ~ 129 Paseo de Pueblo Sur, Taos; 505-751-0365; www.gearingupbikes.com.

Hiking

Within a few miles of downtown Santa Fe and Taos, vast expanses of undulating ridgelines, evergreen forests and lofty granite peaks make for great hiking. Whether your plan calls for a pleasant morning walk in the foothills before the shops open or a week-long backpacking trek into remote alpine wilderness, trail possibilities abound. All distances listed are one way unless otherwise noted. *SANTA FE AREA*   Just outside the city limits of Santa Fe, national forest land beckons to hikers eager to explore the trails that dip around peaks and to mountain lakes.

The **Winsor Trail** (9 to 14 miles) meanders from 7000 to 11,000 feet, sidling along Big Tesuque Creek. Start at the top of Ski Basin Road and traipse through stands of aspen and evergreen and, finally, above timberline to 12,000-foot-plus Santa Fe Baldy. If you prefer a longer hike, begin in Tesuque along the creek. The gentle Borrego Trail branches off of Winsor.

Atalaya Trail starts at a trailhead parking lot near St. John's College on Santa Fe's eastern edge and climbs 2000 feet in less than three miles to the summit of Atalaya Mountain. The higher you climb, the better the view of the city and the desert and mountains that surround it.

SANTA FE TO TAOS Perhaps the most spectacular high-mountain hike in the Sangre de Cristos is the **Truchas Peak Trail** (11 miles), which starts at the Pecos Wilderness portal at Santa Barbara Campground off the High Road to Taos. The long, gradual ascent leads to the long ridgeline connecting the triple peaks of this 13,102-foot mountain where mountain sheep are often seen grazing on the alpine slopes.

TAOS AND THE ENCHANTED CIRCLE Most hiking trails in the Taos area start from the Ski Valley. The ultimate hike is the seven-mile trail to the 13,161-foot summit of Wheeler Peak, New Mexico's highest mountain. Though not particularly steep, the rocky trail is for conditioned hikers only because of the high altitude.

On the Ball

One of the most accessible places to hike or mountain bike close to Santa Fe, the **Dale Ball Trail System** was the brainchild of a retired bank officer who believed that from-your-doorstep hiking trails would enhance the already steep real-estate values of homes in the city's eastern foothills. The network of 22 miles of interconnecting trails that wend through the hills takes in piñon forest, ridgelines, secluded ravines, and sweeping vistas, along with peekaboo glimpses of the backyards of some of Santa Fe's finest

homes. Signs along the way help hikers and bikers navigate the maze of loop trails, which spans the road-less area between two main roads into the mountains.

To reach the northern part of the Dale Ball Trail System, take Hyde Park/Ski Basin Road east for about three miles and watch for the well-marked parking area on your left. Trails run in both directions from there. To reach the southern trail-head, take Cerro Gordo Road or Upper Canyon Road to their intersection near the Randall Davey Audubon Center. The trailhead is just north of the entrance to Santa Fe Canyon Preserve. Dogs must be leashed on the trails and are not permitted on the grounds of the Audubon Center or the wildlife preserve.

The **Carson National Forest** near Taos has more than 20 marked trails of varying difficulty that wind in and around some of the state's more magnificent scenic spots.

Yerba Canyon Trail (4 miles) begins in the aspens and willows, but snakes through fir and spruce trees as you approach the ridge. As its name would suggest, the trail follows Yerba Canyon for most of its length and makes a difficult 3600-foot climb before reaching Lobo

Peak. The trailhead is on Taos Ski Valley Road, a mile up the hill from Upper Cuchilla Campground.

From roughly the same access point as the Yerba Canyon Trail is the **Gavilan Trail** (2.4 miles), a colorful though difficult hike that primarily follows alongside Gavilan Creek. Steep in its early section, the trip flattens out as it opens into meadows near the ridge.

In the Red River area you'll find the trail to **Middle-fork Lake** (2 miles), which climbs 1200 vertical feet to a glacier lake.

Another way to the summit of Wheeler Peak, longer and more difficult than the route from the Taos Ski Valley, the **East Fork Trail** (10 miles) starts from a trailhead near the end of Route 578, the road that serves the vacation cabin area south of Red River.

TRANSPORTATION

Car

Route 25 is the favored north–south road through New Mexico, accessing Las Vegas and Santa Fe. **Route 285/84** heads north from Santa Fe through Española, where **Route 68** branches off and continues to follow the Rio Grande to Taos. For New Mexico road conditions, call 800-432-4269.

Air

Santa Fe does have a municipal airport, but the last commercial service there was discontinued in 2005 because flying directly to or from Santa Fe was much more expensive but not much faster than using **Albuquerque International Sunport**, now the only major commercial passenger terminal in the state. Carriers include America West, American Airlines, Continental Airlines, Delta Air Lines, Frontier Airlines, Great Plains Airlines, Mesa Airlines, Northwest Airlines, Rio Grande Air, Skywest Airlines, Southwest Airlines and United Airlines. ~ 505-244-7700.

Taxis and hotel courtesy vans wait for passengers in front of the airport terminal in Albuquerque. **Santa Fe Shuttle** (505-243-2300, 888-833-2300), **Sandia Shuttle** (505-243-3244, 888-775-5696; www.sandiashuttle.com) and **Herrera Santa Fe Shuttle** (888-833-2300) provide transportation between Albuquerque and Santa Fe. **Twin Hearts Express** (505-751-1201, 800-654-9456) and **Faust's Transportation** (505-758-7359, 888-830-3410) provide transportation between Albuquerque and Taos.

Air charters to Taos are available; contact the **Taos Regional Airport.** ~ 505-758-4995. **Rio Grande Air** provides scheduled service from Taos to Albuquerque. ~ 505-737-9790, 866-880-0464; www.riograndeair.com.

Bus

TNM&O Coaches services Santa Fe and Taos ~ 858 St. Michaels Drive, Santa Fe, 505-471-0008; 1386 Paseo del Pueblo Sur, Taos, 505-758-1144.

Train

Amtrak serves Santa Fe via the village of Lamy, 17 miles from town. ~ 800-872-7245; www.amtrak.com.

Car Rentals

Avis Rent A Car (800-831-2847) has offices at the Santa Fe airport. **Hertz Rent A Car** (800-654-3131) has an office at the airport and in town. **Enterprise Rent A Car** (800-325-8007) offers free shuttle service to its offices near the airport. **Budget Rent A Car** (800-527-0700) has an office in town. If you'd like to rent a car in Taos, try **Enterprise Rent A Car.** ~ 334 Paseo del Pueblo Sur; 505-737-0514, 800-325-8007.

Walking with Artists and Ghosts

Specialty tours are a great way to discover Santa Fe's unique history, traditions and folkways. Most tours last about two to three hours and may include visits to museums or historic buildings. One of the most popular walking tours is Ghostwalks, offered by **Historic Walks of Santa Fe**. Guides introduce you to legends surrounding various Santa Fe buildings, which have far more than their share of phantoms—such as the ghost of Julia Staab, who has been seen over the years by countless guests and employees at La Posada hotel. ~ 100 East San Francisco (in the La Fonda hotel); 505-986-0122; www.historicalwalksofsantafe.com.

At the Palace of the Governors, in the summer and fall, docents guide **Palace Walking History Tours** around the downtown and discuss Santa Fe's history from 1610 to the present. ~ 105 East Palace Avenue; 505-476-5100; www.museumofnewmexico.org.

Another favorite stroll is the **Art Walking Tour** offered every Monday in summer by the Museum of Fine Arts. A museum docent leads visitors around downtown to view murals, outdoor sculptures and the La Fonda Hotel art collection. ~ 107 West Palace Avenue; 505-476-5072; www.museumofnewmexico.org.

Visitors who want to explore beyond the downtown area can sign up for a ride-and-walk **Art Colony Tour** that takes in the Georgia O'Keeffe Museum, Canyon Road, Shidoni Art Foundry, the Santa Fe Opera and other cultural sights. The company also leads all-day trips to Taos. ~ 201 Galisteo Street; 505-466-6146, 505-670-1403.

For information on other walking tours, contact **Aboot About Santa Fe**. ~ Hotel St. Francis lobby, 210 Don Gaspar Avenue; 505-988-2774; www.accesssantafe.com. **Afoot in Santa Fe** conducts two-hour morning jaunts. Fee includes admission to the Loretto Chapel. ~ Inn at Loretto, 211 Old Santa Fe Trail; 505-983-3701.

If you'd like to stroll around Taos with a local guide, call **Taos Historical Walking Tours**. Tours operate in the summer, Monday through Saturday mornings, leaving from the Mabel Dodge Luhan House (240 Morada Lane). ~ phone/fax 505-758-4020.

Public Transit

With their chic tan and turquoise paint jobs designed by local artist Sally Blakemore, the natural gas–propelled **Santa Fe Trails** buses are an excellent way to navigate Santa Fe. Bus #10 takes you from the downtown area to the Indian Arts, Folk Art and Wheelwright museums as well as to St. John's College. Route #2 serves the crop of motels along Cerrillos Road and continues to the Villa Linda Mall, located on the far west side of town. This bus also makes it possible to avoid nasty downtown parking problems by leaving your vehicle at the De Vargas Mall (Guadalupe Street at Paseo de Peralta) and taking a five-minute bus ride downtown. Buses run every half hour from 6:30 a.m. to 10 p.m. weekdays, 8 a.m. to 7:30 p.m. on Saturday on all routes. ~ 505-955-2003, 505-955-2001.

The **Chili Line** bus system provides limited service in Taos only. ~ 505-751-4459.

Taxis

Santa Fe's only taxi service is **Capital City Cab Co.** ~ 505-438-0000. In Taos, call **Faust's Transportation.** ~ 505-758-3410.

2.
The Plaza Area

For nearly three centuries, Santa Fe Plaza was the northern terminus of the Camino Real ("Royal Road"), which linked the Spanish colony of Nuevo Mexico with Mexico City, nearly a thousand miles to the south. In the early 19th century, when Mexico won its independence from Spain and opened its border to trade with the United States, the Plaza also became the end of the Santa Fe Trail, which ran 800 miles from Missouri. Suddenly, Santa Fe's Plaza became the major free-trade zone between the two countries, where manufactured goods from the eastern U.S. were exchanged for gold, silver and—strangely enough—mules from Mexico. The Santa Fe Trail era lasted for about 55 years, during which Santa Fe was transformed from an impoverished frontier colony to one of the most important capitals of the American West.

Today, the Plaza area boasts a heady mix of museums, boutiques, fine dining, art, history and romance. You can learn more about Santa Fe's colorful

colonial past inside the 400-year-old Palace of the Governors, just one of a half-dozen downtown museums you'll want to visit. Be sure to make time for simple strolling—and most of all, shopping. Around the Plaza and along historically artsy Canyon Road, you'll find everything from wooden coyotes and other tourist kitsch to museum-quality Indian pottery and paintings that sell for the same price as a new car.

SIGHTS

There's always plenty of excitement revolving around the Plaza. American Indians roll out their blankets and hawk their wares to tourists on the sidewalks surrounding the Plaza. If you're lucky, there will be live music and dancing. Much of the action focuses on the portal in front of the Palace of the Governors, where Pueblo Indians sell pottery, jewelry and *horno*-baked bread. In the center of the Plaza stands an obelisk erected in 1868 by the territorial legislature to honor U.S. soldiers who had fallen defending New Mexico during the U.S. Civil War. A smaller black granite marker near the southeast corner of the Plaza, across the street from La Fonda, was placed there by the Daughters of the American Republic to mark the end of the Santa Fe Trail. On the south side of the plaza, a gazebo is often used for music and dance performances.

America's oldest public building, the **Palace of the Governors** may be more historically significant than the artifacts it houses. Captured by Pueblo Indians during their bloody 1680 revolt against the Spainards, the 1610 adobe fortress has been used as governmental headquarters for Spain, Mexico and the territorial United States. Today the Palace houses exhibits of fascinating regional history. There's also a working exhibit of antique printing presses, as well as a photograph archive, history library and gift shop. Closed Monday. Admission. ~ 105 West Palace Avenue, on the Plaza; 505-476-5100, fax 505-476-5104; www.palaceofthegovernors.org.

Before leaving the Plaza area, you'll want to pop into **La Fonda Hotel**, which calls itself the "inn at the end of the trail," for a drink in the popular bar or a meal in its impressive dining room. You can glean as much information here about what's going on in town as you can at the chamber of commerce. ~ 100 East San Francisco Street; 505-982-5511, 800-523-5002; www.lafondasanta fe.com, e-mail manager@lafondasantafe.com.

Situated west of the Palace of Governors, the **Museum of Fine Arts** is a prototype of the architectural revival style called Spanish-Pueblo. The building is a reproduction of New Mexico's "Cathedral of the Desert" exhibit at the 1915 Panama-California Exposition in San Diego. Completed in 1917, it embodies aspects of the Spanish mission in the region. Notice the ceilings of split cedar *latillas* and hand-hewn vigas. Housing more than 7000 pieces of art, the museum is a repository for works of early Santa Fe and Taos masters as well as contemporary artists. The museum's **St. Francis Auditorium** boasts walls muraled with scenes of Franciscan monks and their missionary work in the New World. Closed Monday. Admission. ~ 107 West Palace Avenue, on the Plaza;

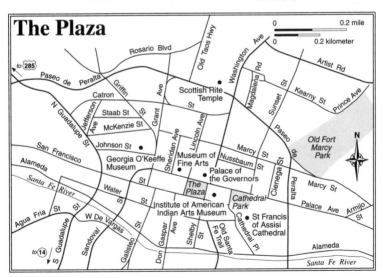

The Plaza

505-476-5072, fax 505-476-5076; www.mfsantafe.org, e-mail ezieselman@mfsantafe.org.

Institute of American Indian Arts Museum

The **Georgia O'Keeffe Museum** occupies three moderately historic buildings connected by hallways in a formerly nondescript part of downtown now known as "the O'K District." You'll find it behind the Eldorado Hotel, three blocks west of the Museum of Fine Arts. Grouped in stark exhibit spaces with otherwise bare white walls and sandstone floors are more than 150 paintings and small sculptures by New Mexico's most celebrated artist, who lived in Santa Fe for the last decade before her death at the age of 90. Closed Wednesday. Admission. ~ 217 Johnson Street; 505-995-0785, fax 505-995-0786; www.okeeffe museum.org, e-mail main@okeeffemuseum.org.

One of Santa Fe's most significant sightseeing highlights is the **Institute of American Indian Arts Museum**. This downtown museum is part of the federally chartered Indian college-level art school (one of only three in the U.S.). Exhibits are arranged to place contemporary

Text continued on page 53.

Canyon Road

Wandering up to **Canyon Road**, you'll pass by historic haciendas and witness firsthand the center of Santa Fe's burgeoning arts community. This shopping district is where the founders of Santa Fe's artist community resided, and in 1935 the first gallery was established (it's no longer there). Early in the 20th century the narrow old river road ran through a low-rent district with secluded compounds of small residences and studios. Now it's an important landmark for artists everywhere. Yet Canyon Road does not flaunt its history, focusing instead on the business at hand: buying and selling art. Zoned for nothing but art, it has the greatest concentration of small galleries in town. High rents have made the old artist-home-studio an anomaly, but a few are still to be found in back alleyways.

Canyon Road features a hundred or more galleries and studios. Sidewalks are narrow and sometimes nonexistent, but the slow one-way vehicle traffic must yield to pedestrians. This is one of the reasons, along with a parking shortage, why it's better to visit Canyon Road on foot. From the Plaza area,

cross to the south side of the river at Paseo de Peralta and look for the big wooden Canyon Road sign. Just walk uphill until you find yourself distracted by beautiful objects. Here is a brief sampling of shops you'll find along the way.

Stunning Southwestern scenes of adobes and more are found at **Ventana Fine Art**. ~ 400 Canyon Road; 505-983-8815; www.ventanafineart.com. The **Hahn Ross Gallery** showcases the whimsical contemporary art—paintings, sculpture, monoprints—of over 20 artists. ~ 409 Canyon Road; 505-984-8434; www.hahnross.com.

Carol LaRoche Gallery has monotypes, abstract and representational art that was created by LaRoche herself as well as sculptures by Ron Allen, Jill Shwaiko Bentz and Allen Wynn. ~ 415 Canyon Road; 505-982-1186; www.laroche-gallery.com.

With much of the selection dating to the 18th century, **Morning Star Gallery** deals exclusively in antique American Indian artwork and artifacts. Museum-quality pueblo pottery is displayed here, along with Plains Indian beadwork, Navajo silverwork and Northwest Coast woodcarvings. Closed Sunday. ~ 513 Canyon Road; 505-982-8187; www.morningstargallery.com.

Take a break from shopping to stroll through the beautiful public gardens at **El Zaguan**, the former home of famed archaeologist Adolph Bandelier. ~ 545 Canyon Road. Then peek into the

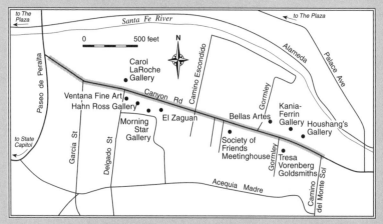

Society of Friends Meetinghouse, which was the live-in studio of Olive Rush, Santa Fe's first recognized woman painter. ~ 630 Canyon Road.

A bit further along is **Bellas Artes**, which features significant works in painting, clay, sculpture, photography and fibers as well as some African and pre-Columbian art. Closed Sunday and Monday. ~ 653 Canyon Road; 505-983-2745; www.bellasartesgallery.com.

Tresa Vorenberg Goldsmiths enjoys a reputation as one of the finest jewelry stores in a city awash with jewelry. Hand-wrought one-of-a-kind pieces are the specialty. Call for winter hours. ~ 656 Canyon Road; 505-988-7215; www.tvgoldsmiths.com.

Nearby, antique American Indian jewelry, basketry and textiles are among the artifacts at **Kania-Ferrin Gallery**. ~ 662 Canyon Road; 505-982-8767.

Houshang's Gallery represents many of the top artists in the Southwest today, including J. D. Challenger, Brad Smith and Nancy Cawdrey, though it tends toward contemporary impressionist paintings. ~ 713 Canyon Road; 505-988-3322, www.houshangart.com. (This elegant gallery has a second location at 235 Don Gaspar Avenue.)

While chic shops line the cul-de-sacs off the lower part of Canyon Road, toward the upper end, narrow alleyways such as **Gypsy Alley** provide access to hidden single-artist studios and small start-up galleries.

The upper end of Canyon Road's gallery district is marked by the end of one-way traffic. Before starting back downhill toward town, take a short detour south on **Camino del Monte Sol** and notice the first five houses on your right. These were the homes of the Cinco Pintores, founders of Santa Fe's art colony in the 1920s, who helped each other build these adobe houses by hand.

artwork within a context of tribal tradition. For instance, located just beyond the main entrance is the welcoming circle, a circular space symbolic of the cycles of nature and the continuity of the American Indian people. Here, before viewing the exhibits, visitors can gather their thoughts in the quiet, contemplative manner in which American Indians have traditionally approached art appreciation. Admission. ~ 108 Cathedral Place; 505-983-1777; www.iaiancad.org, e-mail dcalabaza@iaiancad.org.

The cornerstone for the beautiful **St. Francis of Assisi Cathedral** was laid in 1869 by Archbishop Lamy, a French clergyman from Ohio who was sent to New Mexico to bring the Spanish-dominated Catholic churches of New Mexico into the American mainstream. With its stained-glass windows, bronze panels and smaller Sacrament Chapel, it's certainly the grandest church in the Southwest. In a separate chapel in one corner of the Cathedral is the sacred La Conquistadora ("the Conqueress"), the oldest representation of the Madonna in the United States. Devotion to the woodcarved statue has been maintained for more than 300 years. In the early morning light, La Conquistadora appears positively heavenly. ~ 131 Cathedral Place; 505-982-5619, fax 505-989-1952.

Built in 1911 and situated north of the plaza, the **Scottish Rite Temple** may be familiar to Santa Fe residents but it's a hidden gem to the city's visitors. A tour of the building allows a look at a professional stage, a vintage theater seating area, costumes and a dressing area for the Masons who congregate here twice a year to act out the history of Freemasonry. Closed Saturday and Sunday. ~ 463 Paseo de Peralta; 505-982-4414, fax 505-982-4415.

To take in the whole picture of Santa Fe, hoof it up to the **Cross of the Martyrs**, located in the city's Marcy

Opposite:
St. Francis
of Assisi
Cathedral

Park section. There are stairs by Paseo de Peralta and Washington Avenue that you have to climb to earn the bird's-eye view of the city.

LODGING

La Fonda

100 East San Francisco Street
505-982-5511, 800-523-5002, fax 505-988-2952
www.lafondasantafe.com, e-mail reservations@lafondasanta
    fe.com
167 rooms
ULTRA-DELUXE

Literally the "inn at the end of the Santa Fe Trail," La Fonda hotel is a Santa Fe institution. Though the original 1610 adobe hotel is gone, the latest incarnation still caters to weary travelers in search of pleasant lodging and fine food. Each room is unique, with hand-painted wooden furniture and room accents; many feature balconies and fireplaces. A central meeting spot for area sightseeing tours and recreational activities, La Fonda hums with excitement. A newsstand, an art gallery, shops, a restaurant and a cantina all add to the bustle.

Eldorado Hotel

309 West San Francisco Street
505-988-4455, 800-286-6755, fax 505-995-4555
www.eldoradohotel.com, e-mail rez@eldoradohotel.com
219 rooms
ULTRA-DELUXE

If you find bigger is always better, then be sure to book a room at the looming, yet lovely, Eldorado Hotel. Lovers of classic Santa Fe architecture just about choked when this monolith was constructed. Yet few who venture inside find fault with the brass-and-chrome-fixtured lobby bar, heated rooftop pool, two cocktail lounges and

Victorian Elegance

Tucked away on a tiny side street, **The Madeleine** is a bed and breakfast in a mansion built in 1886 by a local railroad magnate. Surrounded by lush gardens, the inn features stained glass, hand-carved wood trim and Victorian-era antiques throughout. Some of the five spacious guest rooms have brass or four-poster beds, and some have fireplaces. Also on the premises are a tea room and an Indonesian-style spa offering massages, rose petal baths and a Royal Lular treatment, an aromatic treatment originally enjoyed by brides in Java. ~ 106 Faithway Street; 505-982-3465, 888-877-7622, fax 505-982-8572; www.madeleineinn.com, info@madeleineinn.com. ULTRA-DELUXE.

---

adjacent shops. Double rooms are done in a very Southwestern style.

Inn of the Anasazi
113 Washington Avenue
505-988-3030, 800-688-8100, fax 505-988-3277
www.innoftheanasazi.com
59 rooms
ULTRA-DELUXE

You'll love the Inn of the Anasazi's personal touch, from the homemade juice and introduction letter at check-in to the escorted tour of the hotel by a bellman, and thoughtful turn-down service and dimming of bedroom lights. Its understated elegance has made the Anasazi a favorite among well-heeled visitors. Decor throughout the small inn is decidedly low key—neutral tones prevail. Rooms are charmingly bedecked with four-poster beds,

*Inn of the
Anasazi*

viga ceilings, kiva fireplaces, cast-iron furniture, angelic
figurines and handknitted cotton blankets. Instead of "do
not disturb" signs, hotel attendants place leather-tied
blocks over doorknobs.

Hotel Plaza Real

125 Washington Avenue
505-988-4900, 800-279-7325, fax 505-983-9322
www.hotelplazareal.com
56 rooms
DELUXE TO ULTRA-DELUXE

Red-brick coping and windows trimmed in white sig-
nal the traditional Territorial-style architecture of the

Hotel Plaza Real. Situated around a central courtyard, the guest rooms feature massive wood beams and Southwest-style furniture. Nearly all units have a fireplace and most have a patio or balcony. But a word to the wise: Some rooms are small and second-floor units feature steep, narrow staircases. The restaurant serves dinner. Underground hotel parking is $12.

La Posada de Santa Fe
330 East Palace Avenue
505-986-0000, 800-727-5276, fax 505-982-6850
www.laposadadesantafe.com
157 rooms
ULTRA-DELUXE

Guests and staff alike often report sightings of Santa Fe's most notorious phantom, the ghost of Julia Staab, on the grand staircase that ascends from the lobby of La Posada de Santa Fe. The sprawling downtown resort has been expanded over the years to completely surround the mansion of a 19th-century local banker, and while the old house remains Victorian in character, the rest of the hotel blends classic and contemporary Southwestern styles. Luxurious rooms and suites, many with kiva fireplaces, fill not only the main inn but also casitas clustered throughout six acres of beautifully landscaped grounds. There's a large spa facility that includes steam rooms, whirlpools, exercise facilities and a heated outdoor pool.

Hacienda Nicholas
320 East Marcy Street
505-986-1431, 888-321-5123, fax 505-982-8572
www.haciendanicholas.com, e-mail haciendanicholas@aol.com
7 rooms
DELUXE TO ULTRA-DELUXE

Reputed to have been built in 1810 by a Spaniard for his bride, the Hacienda Nicholas exudes old-time Southwest charm. Light and airy, all guest rooms are outfitted with viga ceilings, rustic Mexican furniture and four-poster beds; some have kiva fireplaces and open onto the courtyard. Breakfast and afternoon tea are served in the inn's flower-strewn garden, and an outdoor kiva fireplace provides warmth on chilly days.

Pueblo Indians and the History Museum

For nearly 200 years, Pueblo Indian vendors have been selling their arts and crafts under the portal in front of the Palace of the Governors. Their prices have risen, of course. In the 1940s, the great Pueblo Indian potter Maria Martinez sold her work here for $3 to $5 a pot—now it's sought after by museums and collectors.

In the late 1970s, an Anglo law school graduate who was working as a jeweler while waiting to pass the bar examination filed a lawsuit against the state, claiming that he was being discriminated against because Pueblo Indians were allowed to sell their jewelry under the portal but he was not. To avoid similar charges in the future, the state declared the Pueblo Indians in front of the history museum to be an official museum exhibit.

That's why today the museum regulates the Pueblo Indians who sell under its portal. All items they display must be handmade by the seller or members of their immediate family.

Although the authenticity and quality of their wares is monitored, prices are not, and prices tend to be as high as those charged in the better American Indian arts-and-crafts shops. You get what you pay for, however. Other  American Indian vendors in downtown side streets and restaurants may charge less, but their goods are often mass-produced or of lesser quality.

Grant Corner Inn

122 Grant Avenue
505-983-6678, 800-964-9003, fax 505-983-1526
www.grantcornerinn.com, e-mail info@grantcornerinn.com
8 rooms
DELUXE TO ULTRA-DELUXE

How many different ways can you say sweet? The
Grant Corner Inn is a turn-of-the-20th-century restored
Colonial manor transformed into a wonderful bed and
breakfast famous for its morning repasts. Located next
door to the Georgia O'Keeffe Museum, the Grant Corner
Inn is filled with gorgeous white wrought-iron furnishings, shiny brass beds, handsome quilts, comfy bedding
and an amusing collection of bunny art.

Hotel St. Francis

210 Don Gaspar Avenue
505-983-5700, 800-529-5700, fax 505-989-7690
www.hotelstfrancis.com, e-mail reservations@hotelstfrancis.net
83 rooms
MODERATE TO ULTRA-DELUXE

Afternoon tea attracts a high-tone crowd to the Hotel
St. Francis, one of the prettiest properties in town. Each
room and suite is unique with high ceilings, casement
windows, brass and iron beds and antique furniture.
Original hexagonal tile and porcelain pedestal sinks give
the bathrooms a lush yet historic feel. A spacious lobby
hosts the famous afternoon tea, complete with finger
sandwiches and scones.

DINING

Plaza Restaurant

On the Plaza
505-982-1664
MODERATE

Location is the obvious virtue of the Plaza Restaurant, one of the longest-established restaurants in town. The decor—mirrored walls, red vinyl booths, formica counters—seems not to have changed much since the 1950s, but the food has improved over the years, making it one of the best places to enjoy New Mexican food with an exceptionally nice presentation. The big, garnished bowl of green chile is a full meal in itself.

The Shed

113½ East Palace Avenue
505-982-9030, fax 505-982-0902
www.sfshed.com
closed Sunday
BUDGET TO MODERATE

If a huge old Mexico–style lunch followed by a siesta is what you're after, then seek out The Shed, where wise eaters come before noon to avoid the lines. Blue-corn tortillas wrapped around cheese and onion specialties are served on sizzling plates with *posole* on the side. Consider starting your meal with some fresh mushroom soup and ending it with lemon soufflé. Dinner reservations are recommended.

Inn of the Anasazi

113 Washington Avenue
505-988-3236, 800-688-8100
www.innoftheanasazi.com, e-mail reservations@innofthe
    anasazi.com
Sunday brunch
DELUXE TO ULTRA-DELUXE

Homemade granola and goat's milk yogurt start the day at the Inn of the Anasazi. The innovative kitchen creates indescribable cuisine that blends many elements, flavors, exotic grains and organic ingredients. Homemade breads, seafoods and wild game feature prominently in the menu. The inn's beautiful 92-seat dining room alone is worth a visit.

Now You're Cooking

New Mexican cooking is not Mexican or Tex-Mex. Instead, it springs from the state's Indian culture as adapted by Spanish and Anglo settlers. From flavors to cooking techniques, all dishes are delicately balanced, with the result a literal feast of tastes, textures, smells and colors: green chiles, yellow cheese, blue corn. This mélange dates back hundreds (maybe even thousands) of years. New Mexico's early inhabitants dined on rabbit and venison. But these meats were quickly replaced by beef, *chorizo* (a spicy pork sausage) and mutton after the Spanish arrived. Corn, beans, squash and nuts originated with American Indians. Europeans brought wheat, rice, fruit, onions, garlic and grapes. From Mexico came tomatoes, avocados and chocolate.

Today's New Mexican cooking uses such unusual fruits and vegetables as jicama, chayote (or vegetable pear), *nopales* (the flat green pads of the prickly pear cactus), tomatillos (with their tart lemon flavor) and plantains. Cumin is the predominant spice, though oregano, cilantro, *epazote*, mint, cinnamon and coriander are also utilized.

Traditionalists will tell you there are four basic elements to a true New Mexican meal—chile, corn, cheese and beans. If all four aren't served, you aren't getting an authentic dinner.

One of the best ways to learn all there is about New Mexican cooking is at the **Santa Fe School of Cooking**. Here, expert chefs demonstrate the history and techniques of New Mexico cuisine. Best of all, students get to sample the finished product. ~ 116 West San Francisco Street, Upper Level, Plaza Mercado, Santa Fe; 505-983-4511; www.santafeschoolofcooking. com, e-mail cookin@nets.com.

La Casa Sena

La Casa Sena

125 East Palace Avenue, Sena Plaza
505-988-9232, fax 505-820-2909
www.lacasasena.com, e-mail info@lacasasena.com
DELUXE TO ULTRA-DELUXE.

Considered one of Santa Fe's finest restaurants, La Casa Sena boasts both a main dining room and a smaller cantina. The restaurant, part of a restored 1860 adobe casa, covers its walls with paintings by early Santa Fe masters. Fine, fresh ingredients are used (even the water is from their own well), resulting in fabulous dining adventures. Entrées take regional favorites and give them a creative twist like grilled chorizo-stuffed pork chop, and trout baked in adobe and served with roasted poblano *crema*. Outrageous!

La Casa Sena Cantina

125 East Palace Avenue, Sena Plaza
505-988-9232, fax 505-820-2909
www.lacasasena.com, e-mail info@lacasasena.com
MODERATE TO ULTRA-DELUXE

La Casa Sena Cantina is a bustling crowded space, and everything from food to song is artistically presented. In fact, nowhere else in Santa Fe does the blue-corn chicken enchilada come with a rousing rendition of "Phantom of the Opera" (or whatever the server's in the mood for). The limited seasonal menu includes such specialties as grilled chicken and jack cheese quesadillas with blue cheese, pears, red chile pecans and habañero salsa. Waiters and waitresses perform excerpts from popular musicals, then follow with a sampling of show tunes. Patrons come and go between sets, making their way among the tiny butcher-block tables and baby grand piano.

Paul's

72 West Marcy Street
505-982-8738, 505-982-2090
www.paulsofsantafe.com
closed Sunday
MODERATE TO DELUXE

Paul's
restaurant

This restaurant offers "modern and international" cuisine that is far from simple. Paul's namesake chef Paul Hunsicker serve such delights as grilled sesame chicken with asparagus and oriental vegetables over fettuccini and baked salmon in pecan-herb crust with sorrel cream sauce. There are many fine vegetarian dishes on the menu as well. The restaurant is small, decorated with walls of lively colored folk art.

The Grant

122 Grant Avenue
505-983-6678, fax 505-983-1526
www.grantcornerinn.com, e-mail info@grantcornerinn.com
breakfast Monday through Saturday; Sunday brunch
MODERATE

Though the wait for a table can be long, don't pass up the opportunity to breakfast or brunch at The Grant, an intimate restaurant (it only seats about 30 inside; the 30-seat patio is available when the weather's nice) located within the Grant Corner Inn. While the regular menu has first-rate fare (waffles, egg dishes, soufflés), your best bet is the full brunch special, which includes a fruit frappe, a choice between three entrées, pastries and fresh-ground Colombian coffee or high-end tea. They'll usually have a buffet brunch on holidays. Fresh flowers adorn every table and service is extremely attentive. Reservations are a must!

HIDDEN

Art with Your Coffee

Secluded in an enclosed courtyard reached by an inconspicuous walkway from San Francisco Street one block west of the Plaza, **Tribes Coffee House** serves design-it-yourself salads and assorted deli sandwiches as well as baked goods and gourmet coffee drinks. The hideaway atmosphere offers a welcome refuge from the busy streets of downtown. Paintings by lesser-known artists making their debuts on the Santa Fe scene adorn the walls. ~ 139 West San Francisco Street; 505-982-7948. BUDGET.

Señor Lucky's at the Palace

142 West Palace Avenue
505-982-9891, fax 505-988-7151
www.senorluckys.com
no lunch on Sunday
DELUXE TO ULTRA-DELUXE

A saloon and gambling house had this address in the mid-1800s; now the site has gone upscale as Señor Lucky's, a popular place that pays tribute to its past with saloon-style doors. The eclectic Western menu with regional Southwestern and Mexican specialties includes tortilla-crusted *chile relleno*, grilled Chimayo red chile pork chop, and roasted chicken with achiote tomato sauce. Lime flan and a Mexican chocolate milkshake with coconut macaroons are dessert offerings.

Old House

309 West San Francisco Street
505-988-4455
ULTRA-DELUXE

The massive Eldorado Hotel may be of recent vintage, but it was built on the site of a territorial-era residence and incorporated part of the old walls and foundation; hence the name of its fine dining restaurant, Old House. Dishes such as mustard-and-pepper-crusted rack of lamb are complemented by appetizers like glazed quail breast and chilled carrot-curry vichyssoise. Privacy-seeking diners can reserve the table in the restaurant's wine cellar, surrounded by one of the finest arrays of vintage wines in town.

Fuego
330 East Palace Avenue
505-986-0000
ULTRA-DELUXE

This award-winning restaurant in La Posada de Santa Fe features an elegant Victorian atmosphere, exceptionally attentive service and a Continental menu with dishes you're not likely to find anywhere else in town. If you develop a craving for black cod *en sous-vide*, Scottish woodcock or Texas antelope ribeye steak, this is the place to satiate it.

O'Keeffe Café
217 Johnson Street
505-946-1065
MODERATE TO DELUXE

A cut above most museum cafés, the O'Keeffe Café adjoins the Georgia O'Keeffe Museum. Decorated with photographic mementos of the artist's life in New Mexico, this classy white-tablecloth place serves lunch and dinner in two dining rooms and an outdoor patio shaded by a 150-year-old tree. Typical menu items include organic buffalo filet mignon and smoked Muscovy duck breast in almond cream.

Cafe Paris
31 Burro Alley
505-986-9162
MODERATE TO DELUXE

Hidden away on a tiny street beside the Lensic Performing Arts Center, this little café is half bakery, half gourmet restaurant. The fare ranges from simple soups and salads served with French baguettes to full dinners of beef *bourguignon*, shrimp Provençal or filet mignon with green pepper sauce. The French country atmosphere is as intimate as can be.

PICTURE-PERFECT
Green Chile Restaurants

1. The Shed, p. 60
2. Plaza Restaurant, p. 59
3. Tia Sophia's, p. 69
4. Blue Corn Café, p. 68

Il Piatto
95 West Marcy Street
505-984-1091
BUDGET TO MODERATE

One of the most acclaimed newish restaurants in town, Il Piatto is an authentic Italian eatery with a menu that includes both northern and southern dishes, all featuring homemade pastas and fresh ingredients. A typical lunch entrée is pappardelle pasta with braised duck, caramelized onions and sun-dried tomatoes in a mascarpone sauce. The warm interior is decorated with murals of Tuscany.

Shohko Café
321 Johnson Street
505-983-7288, fax 505-984-1853
no lunch on Saturday and Sunday
MODERATE TO DELUXE

Of the seven Japanese restaurants in Santa Fe, Shohko Café has the freshest seafood and best sushi bar. For a true fusion experience (East meets Southwest), try the green chile tempura. You'll also find ginger beef, yakitori and vegetarian selections. Sake and tempura ice cream are very viable accompaniments.

Coyote Café
132 West Water Street
505-983-1615, fax 505-989-9026
www.coyote-cafe.com, e-mail reservations@coyote-cafe.com
ULTRA-DELUXE

The Coyote Café made a big splash when it first opened and was soon ranked among the top 100 restaurants in the country. The ever-evolving contemporary Southwestern menu typically includes pan-roasted chicken breast and green-chile polenta with black-bean sauce. Some locals feel the Coyote is overrated, but it remains a favorite among the visiting crowd.

Santacafé
231 Washington Avenue
505-984-1788, fax 505-986-0110
www.santacafe.com, e-mail santacafe@aol.com
no lunch on Sunday, but open for Sunday brunch in summer
DELUXE TO ULTRA-DELUXE

My stomach rumbles at the thought of the Santacafé, where herbs are exalted and only the freshest of foods find their way to the table. The combination of flavors never disappoints, from the starter (shiitake and cactus spring rolls, for instance) to the grand finale (chocolate marquise with a cognac creme, anyone?). What's best about Santacafé is it doesn't try too hard when delivering its New American cuisine. Then again, it doesn't have to.

Blue Corn Café
133 West Water Street
505-984-1800, fax 505-984-2104
BUDGET TO MODERATE

A bright, cheerful second-story restaurant in the downtown Plaza Mercado, Blue Corn Café is another favorite. The New Mexican menu covers all the basics (enchiladas, tacos and tamales). Many dishes come with a delicious blue corn *posole* (hominy).

Tia Sophia's
210 West San Francisco Street
505-983-9880
no dinner; closed Sunday
BUDGET

An inexpensive downtown favorite is Tia Sophia's, a long-established restaurant known for its breakfast burrito. This spicy entrée consists of scrambled eggs and chili rolled in a tortilla, a combination that has gained popularity throughout the West. You can't beat the original version pioneered right here. Choose from daily breakfast and lunch specials as well as a wide variety of traditional New Mexican selections. The Southwestern-style decor is bright and homey.

Café Pasqual's
121 Don Gaspar Street
505-983-9340
fax 505-988-4645
www.pasquals.com
DELUXE TO ULTRA-DELUXE

Café Pasqual's is a bustling bistro with some of the most intriguing decorations and inviting dishes in the city. Small and popular, Pasqual's serves breakfast, lunch

and dinner in an atmosphere of Mexican tiles, hanging *piccatas* and lavish hand-painted Oaxacan murals. For breakfast there are quesadillas; lunch favorites include the chicken *mole* enchiladas. The ever-changing menu may include grilled squash and red onion enchiladas with jack cheese or *huevos motuleños* with black beans and a roasted jalapeño salsa. Chocoholics won't want to miss the "killer cake" off the dessert card. Reservations required for dinner.

The Compound Restaurant

653 Canyon Road
505-982-4353, fax 505-982-4868
www.compoundrestaurant.com
no lunch on Saturday and Sunday
ULTRA-DELUXE

Designed by architect Alexander Girard, who is best known for the amazing collection he donated to the Museum of International Folk Art, The Compound Restaurant is where you'll want to go for a very special evening. Foie gras, lamb, duck, caviar and fresh fish are attentively served in this restored hacienda. The impressive wine cellar has some rare vintages.

Geronimo's

724 Canyon Road
505-982-1500
www.geronimorestaurant.com
no lunch on Monday
ULTRA-DELUXE

Serving "eclectic global gourmet," there is almost no culinary territory that Geronimo's won't tread upon. Its menu offers a varied mix of Southwestern and Asian–inspired entrées made exclusively from local, organic sources. There's Colorado lamb chops, New Zealand elk tenderloin and beautiful spicy melon blue crab cakes. The decor is as clean and crisp as the cuisine; the art on the wall and the leather banquettes lend a feel of stunning minimalist.

El Farol

808 Canyon Road
505-983-9912, fax 505-988-3823
www.elfarolsf.com
ULTRA-DELUXE

El Farol has an ambience as good as its food. Hot and cold Spanish *tapas* and entrées are its forte. Try one of the house specialties—paella, cold curry chicken or shrimp sautéed in garlic, lime and sherry—for a filling meal.

SHOPPING

In a city known for its history and architecture, what everyone remembers about Santa Fe is . . . the shopping. Myriad arts-and-crafts shops plus oodles of galleries crowd the Plaza. For a more extensive, though by no means exhaustive, sampling of Santa Fe shopping possibilities, pick up one or more of the book-sized advertising catalogs distributed free in many locations, including *The Santa Fe Catalog, Inside Santa Fe* and *The Essential Guide.* Meanwhile, here's a roundup of a few favorites.

For tribal arts there are numerous choices, including **La Fonda Indian Shop**, which carries quality turquoise and silver jewelry, rugs, kachinas and other Southwestern American Indian arts and crafts in a wide range of prices. ⌐ La Fonda Hotel, 100 East San Francisco Street; 505-

988-2488. Silver and gold buckles shake hands with serpent and leather belts as well as custom-made Western boots at **Tom Taylor Co.** - La Fonda Hotel, 100 East San Francisco Street; 505-984-2231.

Across the street on the east side of the Plaza, **Packards** carries high-quality American Indian collectibles, including one of the best selections of Navajo rugs in town. - 61 Old Santa Fe Trail; 505-983-9241; www.packards-santafe.com.

LewAllen and LewAllen Jewelry has branched out from designer Ross LewAllen's original ear cuffs into pendants, safari bracelets, beading and wildlife-theme wearables. - 105 East Palace Avenue; 505-983-2657.

You'll find old pawn American Indian jewelry, early pottery, artifacts and weavings, along with original 19th-century photographs, photogravures and goldtones of American Indians by Edward S. Curtis, at **The Rainbow Man**, which has been doing business in the same location since the 1940s. - 107 East Palace Avenue; 505-983-8706; www.therainbowman.com.

Go Gallery Hopping

Galleries open new exhibits by hosting receptions, with snacks, wine and an opportunity to meet the artist, on Friday evenings between 5 and 7 p.m. year-round. Listings of the week's receptions are found in the weekly *Santa Fe Reporter* and in the Friday *Pasatiempo* supplement to the *Santa Fe New Mexican*. During the summer months, Canyon Road gallery owners band together to sponsor **Canyon Road Art Walks** featuring refreshments and music on Friday evenings from 5 to 7 p.m.

Even if you're visiting in midsummer, you may wish to drop in at **The Shop—A Christmas Store**, if only to pick up a string or two of red and green chile-shaped Christmas tree lights. ~ 116 East Palace Avenue; 505-983-4823.

Operated by Joseph Sisneros, great-grandson of the Jaramillo pioneer family, **Rancho de Chimayo Collection** features works of Spanish-Colonial and American Indian masters. The collection includes 19th- and 20th-century santero art, Pueblo pottery and contemporary gold and silver, American Indian jewelry, painting and sculpture. ~ In the Sena Plaza, 127 East Palace Avenue; 505-988-4526; www.ranchochimayo.com, e-mail gallery@ ranchochimayo.com.

There is a cluster of galleries along West Palace Avenue between the Plaza and the Georgia O'Keeffe Museum. The **LewAllen Contemporary** is hooked into "the scene" and always worth your time. ~ 129 West Palace Avenue; 505-988-8997; www.lewallencontemporary.com.

Directly across the street, the **Wadle Galleries** exhibit the finest in representational art. Closed Sunday. ~ 128 West Palace Avenue; 505-983-9219.

Important American Modernists, Regionalists and contemporary painters are shown at **Cline Fine Art Gallery**. Closed Sunday. ~ 135 West Palace Avenue; 505-982-5328; www.clinefineart.com.

For outrageous greeting and postcards, try the **Marcy Street Card Shop**. Closed occasionally on Sunday. ~ 75 West Marcy Street; 505-982-5160.

For elegant, contemporary-styled collectible sterling silver bowls and vases from the world-famous factory north of town, visit the **Nambé** factory outlet. ~ 104 West San Francisco Street; 505-9-88-3574.

Among the myriad galleries on the streets surrounding the Plaza, a fascinating place that often goes unnoticed is **Andrew Smith Gallery**. This shop is stacked with limited-edition prints by Ansel Adams, Elliott Porter and many others, including photo portraits of Ernest Hemingway and Albert Einstein. Closed Sunday. ~ 203 West San Francisco Street; 505-984-1234; www.andrew smithgallery.com.

Collected Works is one of the last surviving independent general-interest bookstores, thanks to the owner's careful and thoughtful selection of titles, including an ex-

Global Shopping

The past decade has seen Santa Fe emerge as a collectors market for ethnic art from all over the world. Following is a sampling of Santa Fe's international diversity. **Project Tibet** works with Santa Fe's Tibetan community to aid refugees internationally. The gallery here carries *thankas* (sacred paintings), Buddhist religious objects,

clothing and books. ~ 403 Canyon Road; 505-982-3002. In its hidden second-floor location, **Fourth World Cottage Industries** carries imported handicrafts, textiles and the like from around the world. ~ 102 West San Francisco Street, upstairs; 505-982-4388. Down the hallway is **Alla Books**, the largest Spanish-language bookstore in the United States. ~ 102 West San Francisco Street, upstairs; 505-988-5416. **Origins** is a chic boutique with traditional and designer clothing for women from all over the world. ~ 135 West San Francisco Street; 505-988-2323.

Asian gifts and collectibles are well-represented in Santa Fe. Check out **Shibui Fine Asian Wares & Antiques** for old wooden chests, baskets, prints, ceramics and more. ~ 215 East Palace Avenue; 505-986-1117. Several shops deal in fine oriental rugs, including **Seret & Sons**. ~ 224 Galisteo Street; 505-988-9151.

Rounding out the mix are such unusual shops as **Folk Arts of Poland**. ~ 118 Don Gaspar Avenue; 505-984-9882.

ceptional mystery section. ~ 208-B West San Francisco Street; 505-988-4226.

Glenn Green Galleries specializes in contemporary sculpture, mostly by American Indians, including the legendary Apache artist Allan Houser. ~ 50 East San Francisco Street, second floor; 505-988-4168; www.glenngreengalleries.com.

PICTURE-PERFECT
Art Galleries

1. **Gerald Peters Gallery,** *p. 77*
2. **Nedra Matteucci Galleries,** *p. 77*
3. **Wyeth Hurd Gallery,** *p. 77*
4. **Houshang's Gallery,** *p. 51*

Owings-Dewey Fine Art carries works by classic Santa Fe artists and serves as estate representative for two of the city's leading early painters, William Penhallow Henderson and Will Shuster. Closed Sunday. ~ 76 East San Francisco Street; 505-982-6244; www.owingsdewey.com.

In addition to quality imports from many parts of the world, **Foreign Traders** carries locally made handcrafted furnishings. Its "Hacienda Collection" is created from reclaimed mesquite timbers. ~ 202 Galisteo Street; 505-983-6441; www.foreigntraders.com.

If you're in the market for a fine handmade Panama hat or a fur felt hat, the place to go is **Montecristi Custom Hat Works**, which enjoys a long-standing reputation as the world's finest milliner. ~ 322 McKenzie Street; 505-983-9598; www.montecristihats.com.

For the kid in all of us adults, **Chuck Jones Studio Gallery** carries rare animation storyboards and original animation cels from the late animator and Santa Fe resident Chuck Jones, creator of Bugs Bunny, Daffy Duck, Elmer Fudd, the Roadrunner and Wile E. Coyote. ~ 128 West Water Street; 505-983-5999; www.chuckjones.com.

The Chile Shop has pottery, *ristras*, chile powders and cookbooks. Closed Tuesday from January through March. ~ 109 East Water Street; 505-983-6080.

Find gold jewelry and brilliant earth stones like sugilite at **Spirit of the Earth**. ~ 108 Don Gaspar Street; 505-988-9558. Cotton garments and accessories for women and children fill the shelves at **Pinkoyote**. ~ 220 Shelby Street; 505-984-9911.

Paseo de Peralta is studded with a number of shops and galleries. The **Wyeth Hurd Gallery** (505-989-8380; www.wyethhurd.com) represents N. C. Wyeth, Peter Hurd, Andrew Wyeth, and a dozen other members of this four-generation dynasty of American artists. Closed Sunday. In the same building you'll find **Travel Bug** (505-992-0418), which features the best selection of guidebooks, travel literature and maps in town; it also has a small coffee shop. Also here is **Act 2** (505-983-8585), a vintage clothing store where it's not unusual to find nearly new designer gowns or mint-condition antique apparel. ~ 839 Paseo de Peralta.

Also along Paseo de Peralta, midway between the Plaza and Canyon Road is **Gerald Peters Gallery**, the largest private art gallery in the United States. Its rooms are full of museum-quality 19th- and 20th-century American works by such notables as Frederic Remington and Georgia O'Keeffe. There's also a magical gallery of wildlife art. Closed Sunday. ~ 1011 Paseo de Peralta; 505-954-5700, fax 505-954-5754.

Nearby, the **Nedra Matteucci Galleries** also ranks among the finest in town. Here you'll find works by artists such as early Western landscapists Albert Bierstadt and Thomas Moran as well as paintings by legendary Santa Fe and Taos painters of the 1920s and a secluded one-acre sculpture garden. Closed Sunday. ~ 1075 Paseo de Peralta; 505-982-46311; www.matteucci.com.

Farther north along Paseo de Peralta, the **Laurel Seth Gallery** is run by a second-generation Santa Fe art dealer and carries works by early New Mexico painters, including Santa Fe's famed Cinco Pintores and members of the original Taos art colony, along with contemporary works. Closed Sunday and Monday. ~ 1121 Paseo de Peralta; 505-988-7349; www.sethgallery.com.

NIGHTLIFE

The lounge in **La Fonda Hotel** during happy hour gurgles with the energy of locals and visitors. Hot hors d'oeuvres and music are fine accompaniments to the loaded margaritas. ~ 100 East San Francisco Street; 505-982-5511, fax 505-988-2952; www.lafondasantafe.com.

For a relaxed atmosphere right on the Plaza, go to the **Ore House**. Live music, including blues, folk and country, on Friday and Saturday. ~ 50 Lincoln Avenue; 505-983-8687.

La Casa Sena Cantina has singing waiters and waitresses and one heck of a wine list. ~ 125 East Palace Avenue, Sena Plaza; 505-988-9232.

For a nightcap, try the gracious Victorian bar in **La Posada de Santa Fe** with its chandeliers and leather chairs and cushy couch by the fireplace. If the weather's nice, take a sip on the outdoor patio. ~ 330 East Palace Avenue; 505-986-0000.

If alcohol is not your thing, you can mingle with a sober New Age crowd at the **Longevity Café**, a bar that

Spectacular Theater

With its ornate Mexican Baroque Revival facade, ornamented with fanciful miniature towers and sea monsters, the **Lensic Performing Arts Center** wowed local moviegoers when it opened in 1930 on a site previously occupied by a gambling casino. In most other cities, picture palaces from that era have long since been torn down, but Santa Feans' preservationist attitudes rescued the Lensic from a similar fate. Instead, the Art

Deco interior has been restored to its original opulence and then some. With the renovation, it was converted from a movie theater to a performing arts center.

When exploring downtown, be sure to stop by and check out what's scheduled at the Lensic. It hosts events several times a week, usually at very reasonable admission prices. Performances by the Aspen-Santa Fe Ballet, Santa Fe Pro Musica, the Santa Fe Symphony Orchestra and other local music organizations are held here, as are readings by nationally known authors sponsored by Santa Fe's leading literary grant organization, the Lannan Foundation. Then, too, the Lensic provides a venue for unique groups such as Tibetan monks and the Senegalese National Ballet. ~ 211 West San Francisco Street; 505-988-1234; www.lensic.org.

serves exotic teas and elixers in an atmosphere designed to make you happy, healthy and high. It often hosts consciousness-raising events. ~ 112 West San Francisco Street, second floor; 505-986-0403

A down-home vibe electrifies the mucho macho **Evangelo's**, where the beer is cheap, cheap, cheap. Live music, mostly rock-and-roll, jazz and blues almost every night. Occasional cover. ~ 200 West San Francisco Street; 505-982-9014.

Vanessie of Santa Fe is where the drinks may be among the most expensive in town, but you're in *the* place to see and be seen. Pianist Doug Montgomery, who performs at this upscale piano bar Sunday through Tuesday, is a local celebrity. The rest of the week other entertainers step in and keep the Steinway concert. Gay-friendly. ~ 434 West San Francisco Street; 505-982-9966, fax 505-982-1507.

The Palace Restaurant offers piano music, jazz and other genres every night of the week except Sunday, along with well-poured drinks and reliable service. ~ 142 West Palace Avenue; 505-982-9891; www.palacerestaurant.com.

Santa Fe's classiest nightclub, and the only place where drinks cost more than those at Vanessie, is **Swig**, with its intoxicating decor (the restrooms have faux grass lawns) and amazing deejays. While Santa Fe has no gay bars, Swig attracts a mix of gay and straight patrons, young and middle-aged. Be prepared: it's just about the only establishment in Santa Fe that enforces a dress code—"appropriate attire," whatever that means to the doorman on any given night. ~ 135 West Palace Avenue; 505-955-0400.

On Canyon Road, literally the only nightlife is at **El Farol**, a cantina where locals love to hang out and drink. With a spirit all of its own, El Farol attracts real people (including loads of tourists who have discovered its just-like-real-Santa-Fe ambience). You can hear live music here every night, including flamenco, R&B and jazz. Cover on Wednesday, Friday and Saturday. ~ 808 Canyon Road; 505-983-9912, fax 505-988-3823.

A Panoply of Performing Arts

Music and moonlight fill the **Santa Fe Opera,** one of the country's most famous (and finest) summer opera companies. Blending seasoned classics with exciting premieres, the Opera usually runs from late June through August in the open-air auditorium. Though all of the seats are sheltered, the sides are open and warm clothing and raingear are suggested, since evenings can be cold and/or wet. ~ Route 84/285; 505-986-5900, 800-280-4654, fax 505-995-3030; www.santafeopera.org.

Community theater of the highest order is found at **Santa Fe Playhouse,** the oldest continuously running theater company west of the Mississippi. It offers year-round theatrical entertainment with musicals, comedies, dramas and dance. ~ 142 East De Vargas Street; 505-988-4262.

The **Santa Fe Symphony** performs both traditional and contemporary classical works at Lensic Performing Arts Center from October through May. ~ 211 West San Francisco Street; box office: 505-983-1414, 800-480-1319.

Founded in 1980, the **Santa Fe Pro Musica** performs from September through May at Lensic Performing Arts Center (211 West San Francisco Street) and the Loretto Chapel (211 Old Santa Fe Trail). ~ 505-988-4640, fax 505-984-2501; www.santafepromusica.com.

St. Francis Auditorium (inside the Museum of Fine Arts) and Lensic Performing Arts Center both play host to the **Santa Fe Concert Association** (505-984-8759) and **Santa Fe Chamber Music Festival** (505-983-2075).

PARKS

Located along the north side of St. Francis Cathedral, shady **Cathedral Park** is a long, narrow stretch of grass used on many weekends for arts-and-crafts shows. Virtually ignored the rest of the time, it makes a pleasant retreat from the sometimes-hectic activity of downtown. ~ 131 Cathedral Place.

Nearby, on the other side of Paseo de Peralta, **Tom Macaione Park** is named for an Italian-born painter who was a familiar sight in downtown Santa Fe for decades,

Can You Dig It?

A law requires that before work crews can excavate anywhere in downtown Santa Fe, state archaeologists must be given the chance to examine the site for possible artifacts. In early 2004, when workers were preparing to lay the foundation for the new gazebo on the Plaza, archaeologists sank a six-foot hole to see what was underneath. The Plaza was covered with a two-foot layer of fill dirt in 1972, but between the two-foot- and six-foot-deep levels, the experts found a wealth of Spanish colonial arti-facts including musket balls, rifle flints, military medallions, dinnerware and Majolica pottery.

Even this find paled in comparison to a dig intended for an underground parking garage beside Sweeney Convention Center, begun in late 2004. Archaeologists checking the site turned up ancestral Pueblo artifacts such as painted pottery shards and fragments of woven cloth typical of those found in trash heaps beside ancient Indian pueblos—evidence that a previously un-known Indian pueblo must have stood about two blocks from the Plaza. They also found human skeletal remains from five to eight burials dating to pre-Columbian times. As this book goes to press, construction of the parking garage has been put on hold indefinitely as the archaeologists continue their investigations.

at work with his easel and oil paints set up at the city's most picturesque vantage points. Upon Macaione's death, a near-life-sized bronze statue of him was erected in this small, triangular park. ~ 301 East Marcy Street.

Santa Fe River Park, along the north side of the Santa Fe River, extends the length of the downtown area and beyond. The slender strand of grass shaded by mature cottonwood trees has picnic tables overlooking the river (which rarely has water in it) and a pleasant walkway. Trees along the river that died in the record-breaking drought of 2001–2004 have been carved into sculptures with roots. ~ Alameda Street.

Fort Marcy Park and Magers Field is a large recreation complex featuring an indoor heated pool, a gym and weight room, racquetball courts and a jogging path, as well as baseball and soccer fields. A range of classes including aerobics, yoga, dance and martial arts are offered there. Fort Marcy Park is also the site of numerous community events such as Earth Day and the burning of Zozobra at the beginning of the annual Fiestas de Santa Fe. ~ 490 Washington Avenue; 505-955-2500.

Not to be confused with the complex above, **Old Fort Marcy Park** is a natural area with some picnic tables and a walkway above the Cross of the Martyrs on the mesa overlooking downtown. A popular place to watch the sunset, it was the site of the first U.S. Army fort built when New Mexico was ceded by Mexico to the United States in 1848. ~ Kearney Street at Prince Street.

Patrick Smith Park on Canyon Road is a big, square lawn by the riverside, used in the spring for soccer, in the summer for relaxing on the grass and in the winter for sledding down the small hill at the west end. ~ Canyon Road.

3.

Around
Downtown

Besides the Plaza, Santa Fe's downtown encompasses the cheerfully bureaucratic Capitol area and the shopping-friendly Guadalupe neighborhood, two of the city's designated historic districts. Strict regulations govern every aspect of architecture and construction in these districts. Although new construction is almost constant, often transforming the interiors of former department stores into mazes of small specialty shops, city ordinances dictate the height of buildings, the size of signs, the materials used to pave the streets, the percentage of a building's exterior that can have windows, and many other factors that protect the city's charm from chain stores and blatant commercialism. Except for frequenting the Guadalupe District, few Santa Feans come downtown to shop anymore, but cultural and community events continue to attract locals year-round and keep downtown alive outside of tourist season. With its narrow streets and chronic parking shortage, the Downtown area is best explored on foot.

Capitol Area

On the south side of the Santa Fe River is the oldest part of Old Santa Fe, the Barrio de Analco, which was the living area for Indian laborers brought from Mexico by the conquistadores. Here you can see the city's oldest church, built the same year as the Palace of the Governors (1610). The seat of government moved to this side of the river in 1900, and today most buildings here house state government offices. The state capitol, built in the Zia sun sign shape that graces the state flag, was inspired by the kivas that Pueblo Indians use for ceremonies. All the other sights in the area lie along a short walking-tour route up the Old Santa Fe Trail to the capitol and back via Don Gaspar Avenue.

SIGHTS

Meander up the **Old Santa Fe Trail** through the parklike setting and over the mountain runoff–fed Santa Fe River. Pass by traditional irrigation ditches called *acequias*, which carry moisture from the hills found throughout the city.

Those who believe in miracles must make a point of stopping by the tiny **Loretto Chapel**, patterned after France's Saint Chappelle, which holds the beautiful "miraculous staircase." When the chapel was built, craftsmen failed to install any way to reach the choir loft.

Loretto Chapel

Short on funds, the nuns prayed to Saint Joseph, patron of carpenters, for a solution to the problem. The story goes that a man came armed with only a saw, hammer and hot water to shape the wooden staircase. He worked for months and built a staircase that makes two 360-degree turns but has no visible means of support. When it came time for payment, the man mysteriously disappeared. Admission. ~ 207 Old Santa Fe Trail; 505-982-0092, fax 505-984-7921; www.lorettochapel.com, e-mail information@lorettochapel.com.

The Tlaxcala people from Mexico built the **San Miguel Mission** around 1610, making it the oldest continuously used church in the U.S. But this was probably considered sacred ground before that, as there is evidence of human occupation dating back to A.D. 1300. San Miguel is an amazing archive of everything from pyrographic paintings on buffalo hides and deer skin to a bell from Spain that dates back to 1356. Admission. ~ 401 Old Santa Fe Trail; 505-983-3974.

Tucked away behind San Miguel Mission, the **Lew Wallace Building** is named after the only New Mexico governor to write a bestselling novel while in office—*Ben Hur: A Tale of the Christ* (1880). The building contained the state government printing facilities for many years and now, just as appropriately, houses the offices of the state-published *New Mexico Magazine.* ~ 495 Old Santa Fe Trail; 505-827-7447.

Next door, the **Lamy Building** houses the New Mexico & Santa Fe Visitors Center. One of the oldest buildings in the state government complex, it was originally

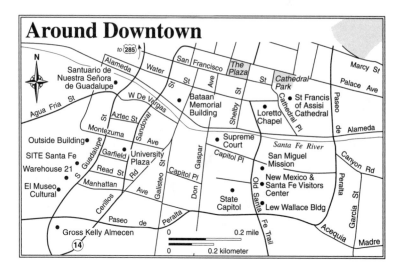

Around Downtown

built by Catholic monks as part of St. Michael's College (now the College of Santa Fe, located on St. Michael's Drive on the south side of the city). It was the tallest building in the city at the time it was built, but the third floor was destroyed by fire. ~ 491 Old Santa Fe Trail; 505-827-7400.

Save time for the **State Capitol**, one of the few round capitol buildings in the United States. Built in the shape of the Pueblo Indian Zia (or sun sign), the three-story structure, with a red-brick roofline and whitewashed trim, symbolizes the circle of life: four winds, four seasons, four directions and four sacred obligations. It also resembles a much larger version of a Pueblo Indian ceremonial kiva. The roundhouse was built in 1966 to replace an older capitol building (now known as the Bataan Memorial Building) down the block. Display cases around the capital rotunda tell the Indian and Spanish history of the

New Mexico State Capitol

state, and you'll find locally made art scattered throughout (the walls are literally covered with artwork). The governor's office has its own gallery, which is open to the public for a viewing reception early in the month. Guided tours of the capitol are available (reservations required during non-summer months). Open weekdays year-round; open Saturday from Memorial Day through Labor Day. ~ Paseo de Peralta and Old Santa Fe Trail; 505-986-4600; www.legis.state.nm.us, e-mail house@state.nm.us.

Across Don Gaspar Avenue from the capitol, the **Bataan Memorial Building** was built as the territorial capitol in 1900 and continued as the state capitol until 1966. It originally had a dome and a columned facade, which were removed when it was renovated in Territorial Revival style in 1951. It now houses various government offices including the Attorney General's office. It is named in memory of the survivors of the 1941 Bataan Death March in the Philippines during World War II, a large percentage of whom were New Mexicans (the New Mexico National Guard had been activated and sent to the Philippines because they spoke Spanish). As a result, New Mexico suffered the highest casualty rate of any state during the war. **New Mexico's Eternal Flame**, near the southwest corner of the building, was handmade by guardsmen before they shipped out. ~ 407 Galisteo Street.

On a grassy slope above the Santa Fe River stands the **Supreme Court Building** (circa 1937), one of the first structures to be designed in the Territorial Revival style that characterizes most government buildings here today. Besides the Supreme Court and Court of Appeals courtrooms and chambers, it houses the three-story state law library, which is open to the public. ~ 237 Don Gaspar Avenue; 505-827-4850.

LODGING

Inn and Spa at Loretto
211 Old Santa Fe Trail
505-988-5531, 800-727-5531, fax 505-984-7988
www.innatloretto.com, e-mail rooms@hotelloretto.com
135 rooms
ULTRA-DELUXE

Adjacent to the Loretto Chapel, the striking Pueblo-style Inn and Spa at Loretto features interior wall murals and Southwest decor that reflect the heritage of New Mexico. Some of the rooms and suites have kiva fireplaces and private balconies. Those looking for mind/body rejuvenation will enjoy the services of the on-site spa. Other amenities include a restaurant with an outdoor terrace.

Garrett's Desert Inn
311 Old Santa Fe Trail
505-982-1851, 800-888-2145, fax 505-989-1647
www.garrettsdesertinn.com, e-mail info@garrettsdesertinn.com
83 rooms
MODERATE

One of the most affordable accommodations in the downtown area, Garrett's Desert Inn is a family-run motel on the south bank of the Santa Fe River just two blocks from the Plaza. The guest rooms, each with a queen- or king-size bed and a private dressing area, are decorated in soft earth tones. There's a heated outdoor swimming pool, a rarity in Santa Fe.

Hotel Santa Fe
1501 Paseo de Peralta
505-982-1200, 800-825-9876, fax 505-984-2211
www.hotelsantafe.com, e-mail stay@hotelsantafe.com
163 rooms
DELUXE TO ULTRA-DELUXE

The scent of piñon wood pervades the polished and contemporary Hotel Santa Fe. Large rooms, many of which have a separate sitting area, are handsomely decorated in those oh-so-familiar Southwestern colors and hand-carved furniture. The first off-site Indian project in the state, the hotel is more than half-owned by the Picuris Indian Pueblo. The Picuris and other American Indians work keep the hotel running.

Inn on the Alameda

303 East Alameda Street
505-984-2121, 800-289-2122, fax 505-986-8325
www.innonthealameda.com, e-mail info@inn-alameda.com
71 rooms
ULTRA-DELUXE

Considering the amount of noise on the street it fronts, guest rooms at the Inn on the Alameda are surprisingly quiet. Everything here feels refreshing, sunny and clean—from the pristine adobe walls to the beautiful slate tiles and the modern artwork. Many guest rooms

Inn on the Alameda

are pleasantly decorated in Southwest style, with wicker and wood-cane furniture; all come with fluffy robes for guest use. Breakfast is included. There's also complimentary wine and cheese in the afternoon.

DINING

Bistro 315
315 Old Santa Fe Trail
505-986-9190
DELUXE

Behind the unpretentious exterior, Bistro 315 characterizes itself as French Provençal but in fact serves an unclassifiable array of nouveau cuisine. Try an appetizer of basil-wrapped shrimp with apricot chutney and curry sauce, followed by an entrée of natural pork tenderloin topped with candied walnuts, braised red cabbage and cassis sauce. It is also one of the few restaurants in town that serves wild (not farm-raised) salmon.

Upper Crust Pizza
329 Old Santa Fe Trail
505-982-0000
MODERATE

Santa Fe's favorite pizza joint, Upper Crust Pizza features whole-wheat crusts and a wide range of mix-and-match ingredients including green chile, feta cheese, pineapple and artichoke hearts. They also serve strombolis and calzones. Grab a seat on the front patio overlooking the Old Santa Fe Trail.

Pink Adobe
406 Old Santa Fe Trail
505-983-7712, fax 505-984-0691
www.thepinkadobe.com, e-mail info@thepinkadobe.com
no lunch on weekends
MODERATE TO DELUXE

Housed in a 300-year-old rose-colored adobe, "The Pink" has been in the restaurant biz since 1944. Southwestern cuisine and Continental-style entrées with a tangy Creole snap dominate the menu, where the favorite entrée is steak served with green chiles and mushrooms. Also tempting is the blue corn cheese enchilada. A selection of tasty desserts, including a French apple pie made with pecans, rounds out the menu.

Red, Green or Christmas?

Ah, yes, the chile: heart and soul of New Mexican cooking. Politics, religion, who'll win the Super Bowl, no topic generates more dispute than red versus green and hot versus mild. New Mexicans consume more chiles per capita than any other state and it's the state's second-largest cash crop. If you were to compare chiles to grapes, New Mexico would be the champagne capital of the world. Local experts estimate more than 35,000 tons are exported within a single year.

The chile (not to be confused with chili powder or chili in a bowl) may have existed as early as 700 B.C. Columbus found "chile" (the Aztec name for the wrinkled, fiery pods) in the West Indies in 1493 and brought them to the New World. Pueblo Indians were growing a mild version along the banks of the Rio Grande when the Spanish arrived in the 1500s.

Nowadays, some still believe a hot dose of chiles will clear the sinuses. True or not, chiles are high in vitamins A and C. Most of us recognize at least a few of the many varieties—green bell pepper, *poblano* (a large, dark green chile), jalapeño, serrano and *chipotle* to name a few. Almost everyone quickly recognizes the New Mexico red chile strung in wreaths and chains called *ristras*.

Members of the nightshade family (which includes tomatoes and potatoes), chiles used before they are ripe are green in color. Once ripe, they turn red. They can be picked and eaten in both stages. Not all chiles are naturally "hot." The amount and variety of chile and whether it is fresh, dried or ground determines the hotness.

Rio Chama Steakhouse

414 Old Santa Fe Trail
505-955-0765
DELUXE

This simple yet elegant restaurant, created by the man who owns the majority of the commercial property in downtown Santa Fe, ranks among the city's finest restaurants. Although it styles itself as a steakhouse, it also serves seafood, lamb and pork, as well as an attractive vegetarian plate made up of a goat cheese *relleño*, grilled vegetables and a mixed vegetable quiche with a green-chile crust. Other house specialties include a fondue generous enough to make a meal for two and a heaping plate of giant onion rings.

Guadalupe Cafe

422 Old Santa Fe Trail
505-982-9762
breakfast, lunch and dinner
MODERATE

Guadalupe Cafe, a longtime local favorite, takes its name from the fact that it used to be on Guadalupe Street. While it serves outstanding New Mexican fare for all meals, it enjoys a reputation for great breakfasts—especially the breakfast tostadas, which come topped with pinto beans, sausage or ham, spinach cream sauce and your choice of eggs, all smothered in red or green chile. A front patio overlooks the Old Santa Fe Trail with its slow, steady flow of vehicle and pedestrian traffic.

NIGHTLIFE

A mix of politicians, tourists and plain old working folks can be found at the **Pink Adobe**, a handsome watering hole located around the corner from the State Capitol. ~ 406 Old Santa Fe Trail; 505-983-7712.

Guadalupe Area Officially known as the Westside-Guadalupe Historic District, the area surrounding the old train station has recently seen more redevelopment than any other part of downtown Santa Fe, and the change is just beginning as the city embarks on an ambitious plan to convert the railyards into a big new park and community complex. The railyards date back to the early 1880s, when spurs of the Atchison, Topeka and Santa Fe Railroad and Denver and Rio Grande Railway arrived. Much of the architecture is markedly different than elsewhere in Santa Fe because the small train station was built in California Mission style, an AT&SF Railroad trademark symbolizing westward expansion. The gracefully curved roofline caught on and was used in many nearby warehouses.

SIGHTS

A recent addition to the city's roster of museums, **SITE Santa Fe** is a private nonprofit "artspace" designed to accommodate traveling art exhibits. Free from the strictures of government-run museums, SITE Santa Fe often presents more daring and progressive shows than can be found elsewhere in town. The vast freeform space—it used to be a warehouse—is flexible enough to fit all kinds of visual-arts exhibits and also hosts nationally known poets and performance artists. Closed Monday and Tuesday. Admission. ~ 1606 Paseo de Peralta; 505-

989-1199, fax 505-989-1188; www.sitesantafe.org, e-mail sitesantafe@sitesantafe.org.

Next door to SITE Santa Fe is **Warehouse 21** (aka the Santa Fe Teen Art Center or the Teen Warehouse), opened in 1990 to provide after-school activities for young people. A full calendar of activities includes workshops and seminars in the arts, from guitar playing and puppetry to photography and deejaying. There are shows and dances most weekend evenings, often featuring local high-school rock and hip-hop bands. Activities are open to visitors, and this is a great place for traveling teens to get away from their parents and meet local kids. ~ 1614 Paseo de Peralta; 505-989-4423.

Across the street from SITE Santa Fe, tucked away in a not-too-obvious location along the railroad tracks, **El Museo Cultural** is a center for Hispanic culture and learning, designed to showcase Hispanic culture, art and traditions. The vast spaces in the 31,000-square-foot converted warehouse are presently underutilized, though the 220-seat theater presents a limited number of programs, and plans call for on-site artist work and exhibit spaces. The facility also hosts the Santa Fe Farmers'

PICTURE-PERFECT
Historic Churches

1. **San Miguel Mission,** *p. 87*
2. **Loretto Chapel,** *p. 85*
3. **Santuario de Nuestra Señora de Guadalupe,** *p. 98*

Market on Saturdays during the winter months. ~ 1615 Paseo de Peralta; 505-827-7750; www.elmuseocultural.org.

One of the most distinctive buildings in the railyards is the muraled, somewhat decrepit-looking **Gross Kelly Almecen** warehouse, which now houses a pottery supply store and artists' studios. It is the oldest Spanish Pueblo Revival-style ("Santa Fe style") commercial building anywhere, built in 1914 by the architect who would later set the standard for the city's unique architectural style by designing the Museum of Fine Arts. ~ Guadalupe Street at Paseo de Peralta.

On the other side of the tracks and at the other end of the Santa Fe architecture spectrum, the **Outside Building**, headquarters of *Outside* magazine, blends components of the city's various styles into a structure as unique as it is graceful. The whole building is constructed around a central basketball court for staff use. ~ 400 Market Street; 505-989-7100; www.outside.com.

Across Guadalupe Street from the railyards, the tallest structure in the area is the mansard-roofed **University Plaza**, an office building that originally housed the University of New Mexico—not the present state university (whose campus is in Albuquerque), but a private school established during the territorial era by fundamentalist missionaries hoping to convert Catholics to their faith. It faced the Catholic St. Michael's College across dairy pastures where the capitol and other state buildings now stand. The school's attempts at "moral education" were not enthusiastically received, and it failed after only three years. ~ 330 Garfield Street.

North of the railyards, the **Santuario de Nuestra Señora de Guadalupe** was built between 1781 and 1807 and is the oldest shrine in the United States dedicated to

Railyards Reborn

The last large tract of open space in the downtown area, the Santa Fe Railyards cover a 50-acre area along Guadalupe Street. Other than the Santa Fe Southern excursion train to the town of Lamy (see Chapter Five), few trains use the railyards today, so the city intends to develop the land as a multi-use park. The planning stages have taken 20 years because ideas submitted by out-of-state architects and developers, which included features such as a supermarket and five-story condominiums, met with strong community opposition and were nixed by the city council. In 1997, the city invited local residents to submit their own plans and brought in a design assistance team from the American Institute of Architects to help prepare the presentation of nine different plans developed by some 200 citizens.

Ground has now been broken on the first stages of the Railyards Park redevelopment plan. It will keep the historic buildings in the railyards, including the old train depot and the Gross Kelly Almacen building (circa 1909), the first "Santa Fe style" structure built in Santa Fe. Another historical feature is the Acequia Madre, the main irrigation ditch that served farms on the outskirts of town for more than three centuries. There will also be a new plaza, walkways, art installations, an apricot orchard and vintage boxcars housing educational displays.

the Virgin of Guadalupe. No longer used as a church (the congregation now uses the much larger Guadalupe Church behind it), it showcases a large oil-on-canvas *reredos,* or altar screen, of the Virgin painted in 1783, as well as a collection of colonial New Mexican *bultos,* or carved wood saint statuettes, and several Italian Renaissance paintings. The Santa Fe Desert Chorale and other music groups use it as a performance space. ~ 100 South Guadalupe Street; 505-988-2027.

Have you ever seen an art museum with only one painting? The **Awakening Museum** is exactly that—a

single vast room housing a monumental spiritual artwork carved and painted on hundreds of wood panels by Jean-Claude Gaugy. You can easily stare at its myriad details for an hour or more. The museum hosts activities designed to foster creativity, trust and tolerance. ~ 125 North Guadalupe Street; 505-989-7636.

DINING

Aztec Café
317 Aztec Street
505-983-9464
www.azteccafe.com
closed at dusk
BUDGET

Caffe latte never tasted so good as in the bohemian atmosphere of the Aztec Café, where you'll find lively conversation, tasty bagels and sandwiches, and art worthy of discussion but, alas, too much cigarette smoke.

Andiamo!

322 Garfield Street
505-995-9595
MODERATE TO DELUXE

Situated on a small side street in a Victorian-era house painted in rich Tuscan reds and yellows, Andiamo! (the name means "let's go") tantalizes diners with such entrées as grilled tuna *puttanesca*, linguini with grilled seafood, olives and capers, and a pizza topped with roasted garlic, fontina, grilled radicchio, pancetta and rosemary. The wine list is long and varied, with wines from Italy, France, the West Coast and New Zealand. Save room for the tiramisu.

Cowgirl Bar-B-Q & Western Grill

319 South Guadalupe Street
505-982-2565
MODERATE

Ultra-casual and boisterous, the Cowgirl Bar-B-Q & Western Grill features artichokes and Texas-style mesquite-

barbecued brisket along with other temptations such as salmon tacos, jerk chicken and supersized T-bone steaks. There are also 12 kinds of beer on tap as well as frozen margaritas and a large assortment of tequilas and mezcals. A kids' play area makes it especially family-friendly. The walls are covered with photos from the National Cowgirl Hall of Fame in Fort Worth. Open late.

Zia Diner
326 South Guadalupe Street
505-988-7008, fax 505-820-7677
BUDGET TO MODERATE

Modern American cuisine in a hip setting with good people-watching makes Zia Diner a fun place to come on your own. Sit at the counter or come with pals and the kids and grab a big table. There's food here for everyone, like meatloaf, burgers, pizza and a Mount Everest–size pile of fries. Breakfast is also served. Zia moves a good crowd through. The Zia bar in the rear hops, too.

Pranzo Italian Grill
540 Montezuma Street
505-984-2645
MODERATE TO DELUXE

A congenial atmosphere and friendly staff put Pranzo Italian Grill at the top of the list of Santa Fe's numerous Italian restaurants. The downstairs restaurant and upstairs bar have traditionally been known as good places to spot celebrities. Creative pastas and pizzas share the menu with more exotic northern cuisine such as a soft-shell crab sandwich and a tantalizing pork Milanese. A special treat is the *antipasto misto* sampler plate, which includes smoked salmon, prosciutto, fontina cheese, grilled portobello mushroom and roasted garlic.

El Tesoro

Sanbusco Market Center, 500 Montezuma Street
505-989-9390
lunch only
BUDGET

El Tesoro, a friendly little Central American café with patio seating inside a mall, is a neighborhood favorite. Offerings include *pupusas* and tamales as well as a more conventional selection of salads and sandwiches.

Ristra

548 Agua Fria Street
505-982-8608
www.ristrarestaurant.com
DELUXE

There's something quintessentially Santa Fean about the mixture of ingredients that make up the widely acclaimed Ristra. Housed in a historic Victorian house stuccoed to look like a Santa Fe–style adobe, its decor blends traditional hanging *ristras* (strings of red chile pods), contemporary tapestries and crisp white tablecloths. The menu, too, is a melange of French-inspired Southwestern flavors. Representative dishes include achiote elk tenderloin and a chile *relleño* stuffed with rabbit and onion confit.

Tomasita's

500 South Guadalupe Street
505-983-5721, fax 505-983-0780
closed Sunday
BUDGET

Housed in an old warehouse and railroad car is Tomasita's, which on the surface looks like a tourist trap. But the food—Tomasita's wins raves for its green chile and *chiles relleños*—and the margaritas wipe away any disparaging thoughts.

Los Mayas

409 West Water Street
505-986-9930
MODERATE

With indoor and outdoor dining in an atmospheric, low-ceilinged adobe building or out back in the large walled courtyard, Los Mayas serves up fine foods from old Mexico. Visitors whose idea of Mexican food is tacos and burritos will find the menu here full of surprises, such as the enchiladas banana (fried banana enchiladas smothered in a chocolatey mole sauce) and the chile *en nogada* (a large poblano chile stuffed with a meat, fruit and nut filling, covered with creamy walnut sauce and pomegranate).

No Esta Aqui

With the unlikely name of **Dave's Not Here**, this great little neighborhood spot serves typical Mexican food and a yummy Greek salad. But the burgers are what keep folks coming back. You can have them with guacamole, green chile, onions or just plain naked. By the way, namesake Dave really isn't here—he sold the restaurant a long time ago. Closed Sunday. ~ 1115 Hickox Street; 505-983-7060. BUDGET.

SHOPPING

The center of shopping in the Guadalupe District is a small mall known as **Sanbusco Market Center**. The historic building, one of the first businesses established when the railroad arrived, used to be a lumberyard named Santa Fe Builders Supply Company, hence the name. Among the businesses housed in Sanbusco, in addition to the Borders bookstore that anchors it, is **Bodhi Bazaar** (505-982-3880), with contemporary casual and dressy clothing for women. Then there's **Kioti** (505-984-9836), featuring elegant women's clothing in velvets and other delicate fabrics imported from Indonesia and China. **Teca Tu** (505-982-9374), a pet store with a difference, carries luxury items for cats and dogs; it does not sell live animals. **Santa Fe Pens** (505-989-4742) offers a vast variety of writing utensils, including antiques and col-

lectibles. ~ 500 Montezuma Street; 505-989-9300.

Adjacent to Sanbusco, **World Market** has gifts, household items and gourmet foods imported from the far corners of the earth. ~ 550 Montezuma Street; 505-955-1700.

There are plenty of other intriguing stores along Guadalupe Street, making it an area where locals are more likely to shop than downtown and where savvy visitors who discover the area can easily get lost for the day. For instance, there's **Cookworks**, a pots-and-pans-and-cappuccino-makers store that has achieved such success over the years that it has expanded into three old brick warehouses. ~ 316, 318 and 322 South Guadalupe Street; 505-988-7676. **Southwest Spanish Craftsman** has been selling handmade New Mexico–style furniture since 1927 and will ship anywhere in the United States and Canada. ~ 328 South Guadalupe Street; 505-982-1767. **Howard Goldsmiths** is among the most elegant and creative custom jewelry designers in the district. ~ 328-E South Guadalupe Street; 505-820-1080. **Rio Bravo Trading Company** carries an array of "American Indian and Western relics—collectible cowboy stuff." ~ 411 South Guadalupe Street; 505-982-0230.

Antique clothing is a specialty in the Guadalupe area. **Double Take Vintage Clothing** features quality retro and designer second-hand clothing, jewelry and accessories, while in the same building **Double Take at the Ranch** has vintage American Indian jewelry and cowboy clothes, including well-broken-in boots. ~ 320 Aztec Street; 505-989-8886. Other vintage fashion shops include **The Beat Goes On**. ~ 333 Montezuma Street; 505-982-7877.

Farther south along Guadalupe Street, a hodgepodge of everything from century-old furniture to original vinyl record albums can be found in **Antique Warehouse**. ~ 530 South Guadalupe Street; 505-984-1159. Nearby, you'll find fresh flowers and a decidedly offbeat selection of greeting cards in an old house shared by **The Flower Market** (505-982-9663) and **Cardrageous** (505-986-5887). ~ Guadalupe Street at Manhattan Street.

The **Santa Fe Farmers' Market** is held every Saturday and Tuesday morning during the warm months in the southeast quadrant of the railyards. Here specialty farmers from all over northern New Mexico come to sell their crops, which range from chile to lavender to all kinds of vegetables, including such unusual items as Russian finger potatoes, dragon beans and oyster mushrooms. There are also homemade jams and salsas, all-natural beauty products and bison steaks. In winter, the Farmers' Market

Spiritual Marketplace

Thriving in the shadow of Borders, the award-winning bookstore **The Ark** carries a smart selection of titles in the realms of metaphysics, holistic health, the wondrous and the just plain weird. There are also good selections of crystals, incense, Tibetan imports and the like, as well as a large section of New Age and world music. The Ark is located well off the beaten track in a hideaway hacienda on a tiny side street; it's easiest to find through its back gate off the railyards near the Outside Building. ~ 133 Romero Street; 505-988-3709; www.arkbooks.com.

is held on Saturdays in El Museo Cultural. ~ Guadalupe Street at Paseo de Peralta; 983-4098.

NIGHTLIFE

WilLee's Blues Club features live music nightly with both local R&B bands and national acts. The long, narrow building has two bars, a stage and always-crowded dance floor and a large outdoor patio. ~ 401 South Guadalupe Street; 505-982-0177; www.willees.com.

The **Cowgirl Hall of Fame**, one of Santa Fe's most popular hangouts after dark, is often selected as the site for wrap parties for motion pictures filmed around Santa Fe. It features live rock and blues bands on weekends (outside on the patio in summer) and singer-songwriters and country-rock karaoke during the week. ~ 319 South Guadalupe Street; 505-982-2565.

The most popular danceclub in town, **The Paramount** used to be primarily a gay and lesbian club, but now draws an eclectic mix of gay and straight clientele. It hosts live entertainers as well. Cover. ~ 331 Sandoval Street; 505-982-8999.

Foremost among Santa Fe's several art movie houses, the **Jean Cocteau Cinema** presents foreign and independent films and has a café area with art exhibitions on the walls. ~ 418 Montezuma Street; 505-988-2711.

4.

Santa Fe's Neighborhoods

With the exception of Museum Hill in the foothills south of Canyon Road, virtually all the familiar guidebook sights of Santa Fe are compactly situated in the Plaza, Canyon Road, Capitol and Guadalupe districts described in the preceding chapters. But Santa Fe is much more than a tourist town, and there is plenty to discover away from the city center in the parts of town where people conduct their daily lives. We'll begin on the East Side, where multimillion-dollar homes share the hillsides with wild evergreen forests in which bears and mountain lions are occasionally seen. Then we'll move to the commercialized and congested West Side, whose primary virtue is that it has nearly all the mid-priced accommodations in town. The North Side centers around the picturesque suburb of Tesuque, where, once you've seen it, you're likely to wish you could live there. Then on to the South Side, a residential area devoid of sightseeing attractions but packed with many of the best (and best-priced) restaurants in town.

East Side East of downtown Santa Fe, the terrain rises into steep, pine-covered foothills and small mountains along the base of the Sangre de Cristos, the highest mountain range in New Mexico. There are no hotels or restaurants in this part of town; it is primarily residential, with custom homes along dirt roadways in the lower hills and gated enclaves of multimillion-dollar houses at higher elevations, giving way abruptly to the evergreen wilderness of Santa Fe National Forest. The main attractions in this part of town are a cluster of state and private museums that can easily take a full day to explore.

SIGHTS

Museum Hill is the name given to a ridgeline complex of two state museums and two privately endowed museums, all celebrating the diversity of cultures in New Mexico and the world. The easiest route for driving to Museum Hill is to go up Canyon Road to Camino del Monte Sol, turn right and drive for about a mile. Buses also run regularly to Museum Hill from the downtown central bus stop on Sherman Street.

The **Museum of International Folk Art** houses the world's largest collection of folk art—130,000 artifacts from all around the globe. Toys, miniatures, textiles and religious art are colorfully displayed in the Girard Wing.

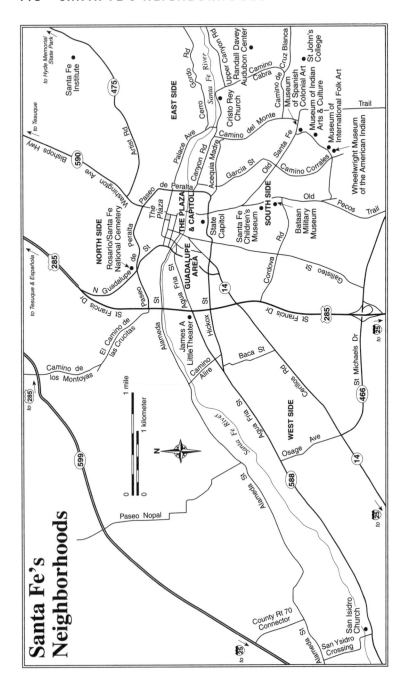

Santa Fe's Neighborhoods

The Hispanic Heritage Wing highlights four centuries of New Mexico's Latino folk culture. Costumes, textiles and quilts number among the exhibits in the Neutrogena Wing and Lloyd's Treasure Chest. The museum plaza, café and parking lot also afford a spectacular view of the Jemez Mountains, southwest of Santa Fe, and the Sangre de Cristos to the north. Closed Monday. Admission. ~ 706 Camino Lejo; 505-476-1200, fax 505-476-1300; www.moifa.org.

Southwestern American Indians are the focus of the **Museum of Indian Arts & Culture**, with exhibits drawn from extensive collections of the museum's Laboratory of Anthropology. Ancient and contemporary pottery is displayed in the Buchsbaum Gallery; exhibits tell the story of 10,000 years of human presence in the Southwest, and a sculpture garden showcases American Indian artists. The library and archives contain countless records, photographs and manuscripts. Docent tours are available. Closed Monday. Admission. ~ 710 Camino Lejo; 505-476-1250, fax 505-476-1330; www.miaclab.org, e-mail info@miaclab.org.

Museum of Indian Arts & Culture

Impressive is a good way to describe the privately owned **Wheelwright Museum of the American Indian**. Though the permanent collection (not available to the public) has a lot of Navajo weavings, changing exhibits feature historic and contemporary American Indian art.

Museum of
Spanish
Colonial Art

~ 704 Camino Lejo; 505-982-4636, 800-607-4636, fax 505-989-7386; www.wheelwright.org, e-mail info@ wheelwright.org.

Inaugurated in 2002, the **Museum of Spanish Colonial Art** boasts a varied collection of more than 3500 pieces that spans five continents and four centuries. Specializing in Spanish Colonial pieces, its rotating and permanent exhibition consists of furniture, paintings, metal work, weaving and pottery, displayed in a historic 1930 adobe designed by John Gaw Meem. There are also creations by 20th-century Hispanic artists on view. Closed Monday. Admission. ~ 750 Camino Lejo; 505-982-2226; www. spanishcolonial.org, e-mail info@spanishcolonial.org.

If you're driving up Canyon Road and, instead of turning right toward Museum Hill where the one-way segment ends, you continue straight, the road will narrow and soon bring you to Alameda Street, where you'll find **Cristo Rey Church**. Don't be deceived by the historic look of this adobe church. It was actually built in 1940 in the style of Spanish Colonial mission churches (such as those in Chimayo, Las Trampas and Truchas on the High Road to Taos) to house a stone altarpiece dating back to 1760. This treasure, one of the finest works of early New Mexican religious sculpture, depicts God and a number of saints. ~ At the corner of Cristo Rey Street and Canyon Road; 505-983-8528, fax 505-992-6836; www.cristorey catholicchurch.org, e-mail cristorey@qwest.net.

A one-block jog to the right on Alameda Street will put you onto Upper Canyon Road, which winds its way up to the **Randall Davey Audubon Center**. The center is named for a painter known for his horse-racing themes. When he died, Davey left his 135-acre estate to the National Audubon Society in 1984. As you stroll the easy walking trails that circle the oak and piñon terrain, you may encounter a wide variety of animal life, including rabbits, skunks, raccoons and deer. Birdwatchers are likely to spot magpies, piñon jays, ravens and dozens of songbird species. A visitors center includes a bookstore with an excellent selection on the natural history of New Mexico. The home, including Davey's studio and an exhibition of his works, opens for tours. ~ 1800 Upper Canyon Road; 505-983-4609, fax 505-983-2355; www. nm.audubon.org.

Upper Canyon Road continues to climb into Santa Fe Canyon, but this watershed area, stretching from the city reservoirs to Santa Fe Lake and nestled in a bowl between 12,000-foot mountains, has been closed to the public since the 1930s. For a scenic return trip from the Audubon Center, take the unpaved but easily navigable **Cerro Gordo Road** back to town. Running high along the hillside, the road takes you past scenic vistas, a pretty riverside park and dramatically situated homes before bringing you to East Palace Avenue.

Getting in Hot Water

Settle into a private hot tub overlooking the mountains under the starlit sky at **Ten Thousand Waves**, located just a few minutes from downtown Santa Fe and set on a hillside among tall ponderosa pines near the national forest boundary. This authentic

Japanese health spa also offers a variety of full-body massages, facials and herbal wraps. There are 11 private outdoor hot tubs, which rent by the hour, as well as a fenced women-only tub and a swimming pool-size, clothing-optional public tub where you can stay all day for a single fee. They're open late, so after a long day of sightseeing, come in for pampering. ~ 3451 Hyde Park Road; 505-982-9304, fax 505-989-5077; www.tenthousandwaves.com, e-mail info@tenthousand waves.com.

If you don't have transportation for a trip to the mountains, you can renew mind, body and spirit right downtown at the **Avanyu Spa** in La Posada de Santa Fe. The original among several Avanyu spas in world-class hotels across the country, it takes its name from the Tewa Pueblo Indian word for the mythical plumed serpent that represents the power of water. Among its many treatments, including facials, body wraps and therapeutic massages, is a unique corn dance purification. ~ 330 East Palace Avenue; 505-986-0000; www.laposadadesantafe.com.

Another first-rate hotel spa that's open to the public, the **ShaNah Spa and Wellness Center** at Bishop's Lodge in Tesuque features Watsu (water massage) and a number of American Indian–inspired treatments, from Native stone massage to the Tesuque clay wrap, as well as yoga, Pilates and tai chi classes. ~ Bishop's Lodge Road; 505-983-6377; www.bishops lodge.com.

If at Cristo Rey Church you follow East Alameda Street until it curves around to become Camino Cabra, you'll come to **St. John's College.** At the entrance to the college is a parking area and trailhead for the popular hike up Atalaya Mountain. The upper reaches of this short (1.5-mile) but steep (climbing from 7500 to 9000 feet elevation) trail afford nonstop panoramic views of the city. For a less strenuous walk in the country, follow the arroyo from the parking area past the college to a nameless, pretty, chamisa-filled valley reserved by the city for future park development.

The other portal to the mountains east of Santa Fe is **Hyde Park/Ski Basin Road,** an extension of Artist Road near downtown (take Washington Street north and turn right). The road passes the **Santa Fe Institute,** a world-class scientific think tank whose members study such topics as chaos theory, scaling laws and cognitive neuroscience. ~ 1399 Hyde Park Road; 505-984-8800; www.santafe.edu.

The road then goes by gated upscale housing developments and the Ten Thousand Waves Japanese baths (see sidebar) before entering **Santa Fe National Forest.** It climbs through ponderosa, aspen and Douglas fir forests, traveling 17 paved miles to the Santa Fe Ski Basin. The ski slopes are normally open from Thanksgiving to the end

Museum Hill Café of March. The rest of the time, the parking area at the end of the road serves the most popular trailhead into the vast Pecos Wilderness, which lies just to the north and east.

DINING

Museum Hill Café
710 Camino Lejo
505-820-1776
lunch only; Sunday brunch
MODERATE

Hues of black, white and brick red accent light the Museum Hill Café, a modern, minimalist eatery set between the folk art and Indian arts museums. Menu choices include an oriental chicken and spinach salad with mandarin oranges and a grilled chicken and pear sandwich.

SHOPPING

With its creaking floorboards and authentic old-time feel, the **Case Trading Post** in the Wheelwright Museum offers one of the best selections of collectible-quality American Indian arts and crafts in town. ~ 704 Camino Lejo; 505-982-4636.

You'll find the **Museum of New Mexico Foundation Shops** in both the Museum of Indian Arts & Culture and the Museum of International Folk Art. The store in the Indian museum has a great range of books on American Indian subjects, as well as a limited but high-quality selection of pottery, jewelry, rugs and kachinas. ~ 710 Camino Lejo; 505-476-1250. The branch in the folk art museum has gift items from all over the world for both kids and grown-ups. ~ 706 Camino Lejo; 505-476-1200.

Case Trading Post

PARKS

Opened in 2002 through the efforts of the Nature Conservancy, the 190-acre **Santa Fe Canyon Nature Preserve** lies along the banks of the Santa Fe River adjacent to the Randall Davey Audubon Center. The river rarely runs through the preserve, since it is dammed into a reservoir just up the canyon, but its underground flow sustains a lush bosque of willows and cottonwoods, which in turn provides a haven for some 140 species of birds. No pets allowed. ~ Cerro Gordo Road at Upper Canyon Road; 505-988-3867.

A long, narrow 350-acre park in the mountains high above Santa Fe, **Hyde Memorial State Park**'s woodsy and sheltered feeling gives visitors the impression they're light years away from the city. This park is a good base for cross-country skiing or hiking in the Santa Fe National Forest. There are picnic areas, restrooms and a sledding hill. Day-use fee, $4 per vehicle. ~ Route 475, about seven miles northeast of Santa Fe; 505-983-7175, fax 505-983-2783.

Camping: There are 43 tent sites, $10 per night; and 7 RV sites with electric hookups, $14 per night. Reservations (mid-May to Memorial Day only): 877-664-7787.

The Sangre de Cristo unit of the 1,589,000-acre **Santa Fe National Forest** encompasses the southernmost part of the Rocky Mountains, including half of the Pecos Wil-

Saturday Night at the Movies

The **St. John's College Film Society** presents vintage films and some contemporary foreign films on Saturday nights at 7 p.m. in the Great Hall at St. John's College. Aimed at students, admission is lower than at other local theaters. ~ 1160 Camino Cruz Blanca; 505-984-6158.

derness, a vast area of alpine meadows and lakes among 12,000-foot peaks. With over 300 miles of trails, the **Pecos Wilderness** area is a favorite destination for hikers and horse and llama packers, while many primitive forest roads outside the wilderness area are popular for mountain biking in summer and cross-country skiing in winter. The main forest access from Santa Fe is the paved Hyde Park/Ski Basin Road, which climbs through the world's largest contiguous aspen forest to an elevation of 10,500 feet at the Santa Fe Ski Basin. The Pecos Wilderness trailhead is on the north edge of the ski area parking lot. The Caja del Rio area is an isolated mesa on the east bank of the Rio Grande across from Bandelier National Monument and the town of White Rock. ~ 1474 Rodeo Road; 505-438-7840, fax 505-438-7834; www.fs.fed.us/r3/sfe.

Camping: Black Canyon Campground has 59 campsites (no hookups); $12 per night. Closed November through March. ~ 505-982-8674.

West Side   The main thoroughfare through Santa Fe's west side, Cerrillos Road was once literally the road to the village of Cerrillos and later part of historic Route 66. Today it is a congested and relatively charmless commercial strip connecting the downtown area with Villa Linda Mall, the city's largest shopping mall. Many visitors find that Cerrillos Road is a focal point of their stay because most of the affordably priced motels and motor inns are there.

SIGHTS

As you drive southwest on Cerrillos Road from the downtown area, you will intersect St. Francis Drive (Route 84-285 to Taos) at the busiest intersection in town. There you'll see the New Mexico School for the Deaf's **James A. Little Theater**, a venue for many live theater and dance performances and public lectures. ~ 1060 Cerrillos Road; 505-476-6429.

A little farther along on the same side of the street is the **Santa Fe Indian School**, originally established by the federal government and now operated by the Indian pueblos of New Mexico. For visitors, the Paolo Soleri Amphitheater, an acoustically sophisticated outdoor bowl with an upswept roof sheltering the stage and an ingenious arrangement of backstage walkways, is quite a sight. In the summer months, it is the most popular music concert venue in Santa Fe and an important source of supplemental income for the Indian school. Soleri, its designer, was a disciple of Frank Lloyd Wright. ~ 1501 Cerrillos Road; 505-989-6300.

If Cerrillos Road traffic gives you a headache, there is an alternative. Several blocks to the north, Agua Fria Street runs more or less parallel to Cerrillos Road. It couldn't be more different. The narrow street, which was once part of the Camino Real ("Royal Road") from old Mexico, goes through a residential neighborhood known simply as the Barrio (which means "suburb," not "slum"), which features a colorful mix of housing that cuts across class boundaries. Like Cerrillos Road, Agua Fria Street was named for the community it led to, but in this case, the **Village of Agua Fria** has been completely surrounded by the City of Santa Fe. In 1995, the village was declared a "traditional historic district," a status that precludes its annexation and urbanization. The centerpiece of Agua Fria village is **San Isidro Church**, a classic white stuccoed adobe church built in 1835, beautifully preserved and still in use. The traditional Fiesta of San Isidro, the pa-

PICTURE-PERFECT
Wildlife Viewing

1. **Randall Davey Audubon Center,** *p. 115*
2. **Santa Fe Canyon Nature Preserve,** *p. 120*
3. **Hyde Memorial State Park,** *p. 120*
4. **Pecos Wilderness,** *p. 121*

tron saint of farmers, is still celebrated here on May 15. ~ 3552 Agua Fria Street; 505-471-0710.

Following Agua Fria Street and then Jemez Road will bring you to Airport Road, where the sole striking sight is the 69-foot-tall, bronze-topped stupa towering over the **Kagyu Shenpen Kunchab Dharma Center**. The center, whose membership is a mix of Tibetan refugees and American Buddhists, sponsors visits by Tibetan teachers, offers chasses in Tibetan art, music and language, and operates a Buddhist bookstore. ~ 3777 KSK Lane; 505-471-1152; www.nobletruth.org.

LODGING

Santa Fe Motel & Inn
510 Cerrillos Road
505-982-1039, 800-930-5002, fax 505-986-1275
23 rooms
www.santafemotelandinn.com
MODERATE TO DELUXE

Not to be confused with the neighboring Hotel Santa Fe, the Santa Fe Motel & Inn has bungalow-style dwellings and standard lodge rooms, some with kitchenettes. Given its prime location, within walking distance of the Plaza, the Santa Fe Motel & Inn is probably the best value for the money. A hot breakfast is included.

El Rey Inn
1862 Cerrillos Road
505-982-1931, 800-521-1349, fax 505-989-9249
www.elreyinnsantafe.com
86 rooms
MODERATE TO DELUXE

The El Rey Inn, with its lush garden property filled with fountains and patios, stands tall against neighboring hotels. Decor varies between Indian pueblo, Victorian and Spanish. Some rooms have oriental rugs; others feature brick floors. Omnipresent in all the units is a keen attention to detail and cleanliness.

Courtyard by Marriott
3347 Cerrillos Road
505-473-2800, 877-233-9330
www.santafecourtyard.com
213 rooms
DELUXE

Courtyard by Marriott boasts a Santa Fe–style lobby in white stucco, dark wood and polished stone with a sitting area by a kiva fireplace. The spacious rooms and suites are more traditional (think chain hotel), with style taking the back seat to convenience. Decorated in strong contemporary colors, each room has a desk, two phones and a free high-speed internet connection.

Stage Coach Motor Inn
3360 Cerrillos Road
505-471-0707
14 rooms
BUDGET

Stage Coach Motor Inn, which used to be a house of
ill repute in the 1940s, features guest rooms that are
nicely refurbished in Santa Fe style with wood beams and
Mexican tiles. The warmly colored rooms at this historic
mom-and-pop motel have two double beds or one
queen-size. One of the suites has a fireplace. All rooms
are nonsmoking.

*Stage Coach
Motor Inn*

DINING

Tecolote Cafe
1203 Cerrillos Road
505-988-1362
no dinner; closed Monday
BUDGET

Breakfast lovers head to the homey little Tecolote
Cafe, which whips up heart-healthy breakfast burritos in
addition to omelettes bursting with gooey filling, and
baskets of biscuits and muffins. Singles sit at a communal table, ideal for meeting local folks. For lunch, the
burgers, enchiladas and burritos are popular.

Cloud Cliff Bakery Café and ArtSpace

1805 2nd Street
505-983-6254, fax 505-986-0205
www.cloudcliff.com, e-mail inbox@cloud
cliff.com
breakfast and lunch only
BUDGET

The artist crowd tends to hang out at the Cloud Cliff Bakery Café and ArtSpace. The main reason is that it's adjacent to Second Street Studios, a large complex where many artists have their workspaces, but the flaky, sweet pastries and inexpensive lunch choices come in a close second. Drop by for breakfast or a light midday meal. Works by local artists serve as decor, a nice touch since most of the workspaces next door are not open to the public.

Mu Du Noodles

1494 Cerrillos Road
505-983-1411
MODERATE

An intimate little pan-Asian place, Mu Du Noodles serves a variety of traditional and novel dishes such as beef *jabantoon*—a melange of seared beef, cilantro, poblano chiles, shallots, peanuts, spinach and other fresh ingredients—or teriyaki citrus-glazed wild salmon. Vegetarians can request to have any dish made without meat, and carb-watchers can order steamed bok choy in place of noodles.

India House

2501 Cerrillos Road
505-471-2651
MODERATE

An oasis of calm beside hectic Cerrillos Road, India House specializes in north Indian tandoori cooking and serves generous dishes such as a lamb *tikka* kabab with chunks of roasted, spiced lamb so big that each one can be cut into four bites. There are also menu offerings and nightly specials for vegetarians.

Tibetans in Santa Fe

Although Santa Fe is widely known for its multicultural character, visitors are often surprised to find Tibetans are part of the mix. Yet if you stay at lodgings on Cerrillos Road, you may well find

that the desk clerk has a Tibetan name. The same is true of other service occupations in restaurants, stores and supermarkets.

In the early 1990s, some of the first Tibetan refugees who were allowed to immigrate from India to the United States settled in Santa Fe because friends of the Dalai Lama lived here. Community support developed quickly, as evidenced by the number of "Free Tibet" bumper stickers seen around town. In 1997, a group of Santa Fe Tibetans was flown to the South American Andes to work as extras in the filming of *Seven Years in Tibet.* The same year, the **Tibetan Association of Santa Fe** was formed to preserve Tibetan culture, language and religion. ~ P.O. Box 2651, Santa Fe, NM 87505; e-mail lamagyaltsen@aol.com.

To learn more about Tibetans in Santa Fe, visit **Project Tibet.** ~ 403 Canyon Road; 505-982-3002. Or drop by the **Noble Truth Bookstore** at the Kagyu Shenpen Kunchab Dharma Center. ~ 3777 KSK Lane; 505-471-1152.

Bert's La Taqueria
1620 St. Michael's Drive
505-474-0791
MODERATE

Just off Cerrillos Road in the St. Michael's Village Shopping Center, Bert's La Taqueria serves stacks of soft, warm flour tortillas with a heap of your choice of ingredients—chicken, shrimp or shredded beef, to name a few—and a spread of different salsas. The chef also offers

up gourmet Mexican specials. The atmosphere tends to be boisterous at this popular neighborhood eatery.

SHOPPING

For American Indian arts, try **Tin-Nee-Ann**, which specializes in Southwestern arts and crafts. Closed Sunday. ~ 923 Cerrillos Road; 505-988-1630.

Just about every Santa Fe home contains an item of decor from **Jackalope**, one of the most unusual shopping spots in town. Far from the chic shops of the Plaza and Canyon Road, the huge store sprawls across a six-square-block tract of the city's westside motel strip. Living up to its slogan of "Folk Art by the Truckload," the complex shows off the heaps of pottery, Spanish colonial furniture, handmade clothing and other wares that have made it the largest Mexican import retailer in the United States. You'll also find buildings full of antiques and exotica from India and Bali, as well as an outdoor cantina with live music and a prairie dog enclosure. It's the closest thing to a theme park in Santa Fe, and admission is free. ~ 2820 Cerrillos Road; 505-471-8539, fax 505-471-6710; www.jackalope.com.

NIGHTLIFE

The beautiful Paolo Soleri Outdoor Theater of the Santa Fe Indian School campus serves as home to the **Santa Fe Summer Concert Series**, which brings big-name acts to town May through September. ~ On campus of the Santa Fe Indian School, 1501 Cerrillos Road; 505-989-6320.

Get ready to kick up your heels at **Rodeo Nites**, a rowdy nightclub for lovers of country-and-western music.

Live bands play nightly: country bands entertain Friday, *Nuevo Mexicano* groups perform on Thursday and Saturday, and big-name Mexican outfits take the stage on Sunday. Cover Thursday through Sunday. Closed Monday through Wednesday. ~ 2911 Cerrillos Road; 505-473-4138.

You'll find a cross-section of the whole community at **Club Alegría**, which features local *norteño* (Mexican cowboy) bands along with salsa music and Tex-Mex country-and-western. The big event comes on the last Friday of each month, when Father Frank Pretto, the "salsa priest" (and pastor of San Isidro Church in the village of Agua Fria), cuts loose with his band's hot Latin rhythms. ~ 2797 Agua Fria Street; 505-471-2324.

Part of the College of Santa Fe's multimillion-dollar Moving Images film arts facility donated by actress Greer Garson, **The Screen** has public showings of foreign and independent films as well as vintage and rarely seen Hollywood pictures. It is the largest movie screen in Santa Fe. ~ 1600 St. Michael's Drive; 505-473-6494.

PARKS

There has been a long-running controversy in Santa Fe over whether to exterminate or tolerate prairie dogs in the city parks. At **Frenchy's Field Park**, the prairie dogs have definitely won. A former dairy farm, the park has a broad pasture surrounded by a one-third-mile paved walking track, surrounding a colony of hundreds of prairie dogs. Wildflowers are colorful here in late summer. The park also has picnic tables, a goldfish pond and a community-built adobe labyrinth. ~ Agua Fria Street at Osage Street.

North Side
Growth on the city's north side is largely inhibited by lack of water and by the proximity of tribal lands. The most striking exception is the village of Tesuque, where you can drive along a country lane so picture-perfect that it seems to embody all the romanticism of rural Santa Fe county. Along the way you'll find a unique park where huge sculptures destined for places of honor in front of big-city skyscrapers are exhibited and sold.

SIGHTS

Just north of Rosario Cemetery along Guadalupe Street, neat rows and columns of white grave markers fill the **Santa Fe National Cemetery**, the last resting place of many U.S. military veterans. ~ 501 North Guadalupe Street; 505-988-6400.

North of downtown Santa Fe (follow Washington Street, which becomes Bishop's Lodge Road) is the picturesque valley of Tesuque, perhaps the most romantic neighborhood in town, a mixed community of celebri-

The Virgin Mary's Summer Home

In Santa Fe's main Catholic cemetery, across from the De Vargas Mall, stands **Rosario Chapel**, the least known of Santa Fe's historic churches. With its beautiful stained-glass windows, it dates back to 1807, near the end of the Spanish Colonial era, and was built to house La Conquistadora. Although the statuette of the Virgin Mary now "lives" in a special chapel within St. Francis Cathedral, each summer her *cofradia* of attendants take her on a "pilgrimage" procession to Rosario Chapel, where she presides over nine masses before returning in another procession to the cathedral. ~ North Paseo de Peralta and Guadalupe Street; 505-983-2322.

*Bishop
Lamy's
chapel*

ties and the ultra-wealthy living in adobe mansions alongside artists, writers and healers housed in cozy little creekside guesthouses.

Visit Archbishop Lamy's private chapel at the **Bishop's Lodge**. Small, private and very holy are words that characterize this sanctuary along the Little Tesuque Stream. *Vigas* have replaced the former rafters in this intimate chapel, but the archbishop's cloak, hat and crucifix remain. Enter by way of an old church key! It's quite possible that a visit here will inspire you to read Willa Cather's classic, *Death Comes for the Archbishop*. ~ Bishop's Lodge Road, Santa Fe; 505-983-6377; www.bishopslodge.com, e-mail bishopslodge@bishopslodge.com.

As far as art galleries go, none is quite like the **Shidoni Foundry**, where bronze pourings take place on Saturdays. The art foundry, gardens and contemporary gallery are world-renowned among purveyors of fine art. You can experience Shidoni's charm with a stroll through the foundry's two large, peaceful parks, where dozens of metal sculptures—many of them monumental in size and price—await corporate buyers. Closed Sunday. ~ Bishop's Lodge Road, Tesuque; 505-988-8001, fax 505-984-8115; www.shidoni.com, e-mail shidoni@shidoni.com.

The **Santa Fe Opera** enjoys an international reputation because of its world-class talent, lavish costumes and sets, apprentice program (where many leading singers get their start) and its willingness to premiere contemporary operas by American composers alongside more traditional fare. The opera was originally built as an open-air theater; founder John Crosby first visited Santa Fe during a drought and did not realize that during the July-through-August opera season thunderstorms normally come every day. In 1997, a roof was placed over the theater with a suspension system so elaborate it looks like a flying machine. Backstage tours through the costume and production areas are offered every Saturday at 1 p.m. during opera season. ~ Seven miles north of Santa Fe on Route 84/285; 505-986-5955, 800-280-4654; www. santafeopera.org.

LODGING

Radisson Santa Fe

750 North St. Francis Drive
505-992-5800; 800-333-3333
www.radisson.com/santafenm
141 rooms
DELUXE

Set on a hillside with great views of the Sangre de
Cristo Mountains and . . . well . . . the National Cemetery,
the Radisson offers spacious, contemporary guest rooms
and suites. Facilities include a 20,000-square-foot spa and
exercise area as well as an outdoor swimming pool in its
landscaped courtyard. Shuttles run downtown on a regular basis and also take guests out to the opera on performance nights.

Bishop's Lodge

Bishop's Lodge Road
505-983-6377, 800-732-2240, fax 505-989-8739
www.bishopslodge.com, e-mail bishopslodge@bishopslodge.com
111 rooms
ULTRA-DELUXE

Another rather rural alternative to the city lodging experience, The Bishop's Lodge is steeped in a rich history.
The property along the Little Tesuque Stream was once
the private retreat of Archbishop Jean Baptiste Lamy. The
bishop's sacred, private chapel still stands behind the
main lodge and can be entered by borrowing a special
key from the front desk. Since 1917, the 440-acre ranch
has hosted guests who may choose to pursue a variety of
activities, including horseback riding, swimming, medi-
tative hikes and tennis. Well-kept guest rooms are decorated in ranch motif, while a spa and wellness center is
also available.

DINING

Banana Café
329 West San Francisco Street
505-982-3886
BUDGET TO MODERATE

Originally a Thai restaurant, the Banana Café broadened its fare to include Chinese and other Asian cuisine. The spicy coconut curry dishes still rank among the top offerings, as does the basil-lemongrass chicken. The decor is exotic, with elaborate wood carvings, faux flames and handcrafted screens that divide up the dining areas.

Bumble Bee's Baja Grill
301 Jefferson Street
505-820-2862
BUDGET

The owners of Bumble Bee's Baja Grill originally wanted to open a location of California's Baja Fresh chain in Santa Fe, but their application was turned down because corporate headquarters deemed this city of 100,000

"Love Feast" by Milton Hebald at Shidoni Foundry

Going to the Dogs

Like most cities, Santa Fe has a leash law, so if you're traveling with a canine companion, you'll want to search out what may be Santa Fe's best-hidden park, **Frank Ortiz Park**, where dogs are allowed to run free. Your pet will get a chance to play with local dogs and, if you wish, you'll have plenty of opportunity to meet the locals as well. (If you're asking for directions, locals just call it the "dog park.") To get there, from Guadalupe Street or Route 84/285, turn west on Alamo Street near the Radisson Santa Fe, then turn right at the traffic roundabout and follow Camino de las Crucitas to the top of the hill.

The dog park has miles of walking trails along juniper-covered ridgelines with impressive views of the city, as well as a broad, flat, barren play area the size of half-a-dozen football fields. A monument near the park entrance explains that this was originally the site of a World War II Japanese-American internment camp, which was demolished after the war and converted into a landfill. When the dump was full, it was covered over, graded and made into the park that's there today. Frank Ortiz, for whom the park was named, was a native Santa Fean who served for 40 years as a U.S. ambassador in Guatemala, Peru and Argentina. ~ Camino de las Crucitas; 505-955-2106.

too small. So they decided to open their own independent, improved version. The atmosphere is fast-food take-out, but the ingredients are all fresh, the chef is a New York–trained veteran of some of Santa Fe's finest restaurants, and the bill of fare features mahimahi tacos and great grilled steak burritos. Nothing on the menu is fried.

Santa Fe Bar & Grill
In the De Vargas Mall, 187 Paseo de Peralta
505-982-3033
www.santafebargrill.com
MODERATE

A hand-tooled bar from Puebla, Mexico, a stamped tin ceiling and a backbar made from old mesquite doors, along with antique pots and pans and an open kitchen, set the stage for the fine New Mexican food served at Santa Fe Bar & Grill. Whole chickens sizzle on the rotisserie, and nouveau cuisine showcases traditional local ingredients such as squash, corn, pinto beans, chiles, cilantro and garlic. You'll also find steaks and seafood on the menu. Local and regional microbrews and wines are served.

Jinja
510 North Guadalupe Street
505-982-4321
MODERATE

Dim lighting, black lacquer and throw pillows create the mood at Jinja, an Asian nouveau restaurant. Try a cup of the Thai-style coconut-shrimp soup followed by the rice paper baked wild salmon at this neighborhood favorite. Sip jasmine tea or pear *sake*, and leave room for a wedge of lemon-lime tart with sorbet for dessert.

Las Fuentes at Bishop's Lodge
Bishop's Lodge Road
505-983-6377
Sunday brunch
ULTRA-DELUXE

Chic Country Cafe

Before it gets any trendier, check out the **Tesuque Village Market** and its casually chic atmosphere. The Tesuque chile-cheeseburger, stir-fry veggie plate and salads are highly recommended. There's a full wine cellar and good choices by the glass. ~ Route 591 and Bishop's Lodge Road, Tesuque; 505-988-8848, fax 505-986-0921. BUDGET TO MODERATE.

Las Fuentes at Bishop's Lodge, an elegant restaurant at the big country resort north of Santa Fe, features such gourmet menu choices as New Mexico green chile crab cakes; espresso and red chile dusted buffalo steak; and paillard of Malaysian *monchong* (a delicacy also known as "utopia fish") on a ragoût of Australian rock shrimp and parsnips. Santa Feans flock to Bishop's Lodge on Sunday for the lavish all-you-can-eat brunch.

NIGHTLIFE

The sizzling **Teatro Flamenco** returns to Santa Fe each summer (late June through August) for a series of flamenco dance concerts under the direction of Maria Benitez. Performances are held at the Radisson Santa Fe (750 North St. Francis Drive). ~ 505-955-8562, 888-435-2636; www.mariabenitez.com.

South Side The predominantly residential south side of Santa Fe, anchored between the massive office buildings of the South Capital Complex and the sprawling St. Vincent's Hospital and surrounding medical buildings, has little to offer in the way of sightseeing. It's good to know about, though, because some of the best restaurants in town—the ones where locals take out-of-town guests but most tourists never discover on their own—are located here.

SIGHTS

If you're traveling with kids, consider a stop at the **Santa Fe Children's Museum**. Budding architects can design and build a room from PVC pipes, young musicians can compose original tunes on an assortment of xylophones and future physicists can marvel at the echoing sound dishes. Earthworks, an educational, one-acre garden, harbors a greenhouse, wetlands and hummingbird and butterfly gardens. Closed Monday and Tuesday. Admission. ~ 1050 Old Pecos Trail; 505-989-8359, fax 505-989-7506; www.santafechildrensmuseum.org, e-mail children@santafechildrensmuseum.org.

Military memorabilia seem strangely out of place in Santa Fe, but the **Bataan Military Museum**, housed in the former National Guard Armory, has plenty of it. You'll find items dating from World War I through the first Gulf War, with an emphasis on the Bataan Death March, which claimed the lives of many New Mexicans in the Philippines during World War II. The museum has over 30,000 artifacts as well as a large archive of military documents. Closed Sunday and Monday. ~ 1050 Old Pecos Trail; 505-474-1670.

The **School of American Research**, the successor to the School of American Archaeology that occupied and restored the Palace of the Governors in the early years of the 20th century, is now housed in a sprawling mansion donated by local benefactress Amelia White in 1972. The school is in the forefront of studying pre-Columbian Indian archaeological sites both in the Southwest and in the Maya regions of Mexico and Central America. It is open to the public only on Friday afternoons, when tours are available by advance reservation to see the best of the

SAR's collection of more than 10,000 artifacts and its extensive library. ~ 660 Garcia Street; 505-954-7200, fax 505-989-9809; www.sarweb.org.

LODGING

Las Brisas de Santa Fe
624 Galisteo Street
505-982-5795, 800-449-6231, fax 505-982-7900
www.lasbrisasdesantafe.com, e-mail lasbrisas@cybermesa.com
10 condos
ULTRA-DELUXE

Providing some of the most luxurious lodging in town, Las Brisas de Santa Fe offers *viga* ceilings and kiva fireplaces (stocked with plenty of wood) in its Santa Fe–style adobe units. Choose between one and two bedrooms, both of which have queen- or king-size beds and fully equipped kitchens. If it's a warm night, you can enjoy dinner on your private patio. Located eight blocks from

Sleeping with Poets

The **Inn of the Turquoise Bear** is located in a secluded southside adobe mansion that originally belonged to poet/philanthropist Witter Bynner, a leader of Santa Fe's literary community for four decades beginning in the Roaring Twenties. Among the many luminaries who stayed here as Bynner's houseguests were composer Igor Stravinsky, poet Robert Frost, actors Errol Flynn and Rita Hayworth, and playwright Thornton Wilder. Each of the ten guest rooms has traditional Santa Fe–style decor and modern amenities from VCRs to terry-cloth robes and fresh, fragrant flowers. The inn is pleasantly shaded by lofty ponderosa pines on an acre of grounds with terraced gardens, old stone benches and flagstone footpaths. Gay-friendly. ~ 342 East Buena Vista Street; 505-983-0798, 800-396-4104, fax 505-988-4225; www.turquoisebear.com, e-mail bluebear@newmexico.com. MODERATE TO ULTRA-DELUXE.

the downtown plaza in a compound on a quiet residential side street, these time-share condominiums rent by the night, so the number of units available varies seasonally.

Pecos Trail Inn

2239 Old Pecos Trail
505-982-1943, 800-304-4187
www.pecostrailinn.com
22 rooms
MODERATE

Contemporary artwork on the walls, massive Mexican furnishings, saltillo tile floors and decorative *nichos* carved into soft-hued off-white walls set the Pecos Trail Inn apart from run-of-the-mill motels. Nestled against a hillside covered with piñon forest, this pet-friendly establishment is the only motel in the vicinity, convenient to the Old Pecos Trail exit from Route 25 and an easy ten-minute drive from downtown.

DINING

La Choza

905 Alarid Street
505-982-0909
MODERATE

Everybody has heard of the downtown restaurant The Shed, where celebs like Bill Clinton and Teresa Heinz Kerry sample local chile when they're in town. But few visitors know about La Choza (Spanish for "The Shed"), which is owned by the same family and serves the same classic New Mexico–style enchiladas, fajitas and stuffed *sopapillas* in a friendly, neighborhood setting. Locals love it. Look for it near the northeast corner of the intersection of Cerrillos Road and St. Francis Drive.

Tiny's
1015 Pen Road
505-983-9817
MODERATE

Tiny's is another long-established local chile eatery, hidden away at the back of the Pen Shopping Center near the southeast corner of Cerrillos Road and St. Francis Drive. The no-nonsense menu features chicken enchiladas, vegetarian burritos and green-chile cheeseburgers. The spacious dining areas surround a comfortable central courtyard.

Mariscos "La Playa"
537 Cordova Road
505-982-2790
MODERATE

Mariscos "La Playa" has all the funky charm of a tropical beachfront eatery, right down to the lacy paper cutouts hanging from the ceiling and the Corona beer signs on the walls, plus a mural showing sunbathers and parasailers on a wave-lapped white-sand beach. Outstandingly tasty and reasonably priced, the food at this family-run Mexican seafood restaurant is as authentic as can be, from *camarones al mojo de ajo* (shrimp in garlic sauce) to *huachinango veracruzano* (red snapper in a spicy salsa).

Santa Fe Baking Company
504 West Cordova Road
505-988-4292
breakfast, lunch and dinner
BUDGET

Noisy, often crowded, and always friendly, the Santa Fe Baking Company is frequented by artists and healers, South Capital bureaucrats, and lots of laptop lingerers taking advantage of the free wireless internet hookup. A great place to meet the locals, this neighborhood hang-

Can You Say "Comida"?

Before ordering in a New Mexican restaurant, it's a good idea to master a few Spanish terms for the basic dishes. For example, *carne asada* means roasted meat (though it now sometimes includes grilled meat). *Carne adovada* refers to meat marinated in red chile. Chicken in chile sauce is known as *mole*.

A traditional tamale is a combination of minced meat and red pepper rolled in corn meal, wrapped in corn husks and baked or steamed. The ever-popular *chiles relleños* refers to a large, battered, fried green chile, stuffed with cheese, avocado, shrimp, pork, etc. *Chile con queso* is a chile and cheese pie. A side order of *frijoles* will get you a plate of pinto beans. *Sopapilla* translates to "pillow," an apt description for the light, puffy fried dough typically served drizzled with honey.

Tortillas are the "bread" of New Mexico. Usually made of white cornmeal, they come hot and fresh with almost every dish. Some cooks favor flour or blue cornmeal for preparing tortillas. And yes, blue corn is really "blue." Finally, you should never be embarrassed to ask questions or request your chile on the side. New Mexicans take great pride in their colorful cuisine and want you to enjoy all the magnificent flavors it holds.

out is especially popular for breakfast, when the fare includes a tasty breakfast burrito and one of the best plates of *huevos rancheros* (fried eggs on tortillas, smothered in green chile) in town. Lunch and dinner are also served.

Maria's New Mexican Kitchen

555 West Cordova Road
505-983-7929
www.marias-santafe.com
BUDGET TO MODERATE

Many locals contend that Maria's is the ultimate northern New Mexico restaurant. It has operated in the same location since 1952. The 30-entrée menu features

PICTURE-PERFECT
Locals' Favorite Restaurants

1. **Maria's New Mexican Kitchen**, *p. 143*
2. **Cloud Cliff Bakery Café and ArtSpace**, *p. 126*
3. **Chow's**, *p. 144*
4. **Tesuque Village Market**, *p. 137*

blue-corn enchiladas, fajitas and steaks, as well as a combination plate with a cheese enchilada, a taco, a tamale and a *chile relleño*. But the restaurant is most renowned for its margaritas—100 different kinds—made with fine tequilas from the state of Jalisco, Mexico, and a variety of fresh fruits including limes, peaches and strawberries. The bar features murals by artist Alfred Morang, done in exchange for food and drink.

Chow's

720 St. Michaels Drive
505-471-7120
www.mychows.com
MODERATE

Located behind a Kinko's in a small shopping center, this spotlessly clean restaurant serves contemporary Chinese food—wok-cooked but unlike anything you'd expect of an ordinary Chinese restaurant. Try the firecracker dumplings (dumplings stuffed with carrots, ground turkey and chile in a pesto sauce), scallops stir-fried with red peppers in coconut sauce, or nuts and birds (chicken and water chestnuts stir-fried with zucchini in a Szechuan sauce). For dessert, try the green tea ice cream.

Chocolate Maven
821 San Mateo Road
505-984-1980
Saturday and Sunday brunch; no dinner
BUDGET TO MODERATE

Chocolate Maven is primarily a dessert bakery, and an amazing one at that. The owners report that they go through nearly 14,000 pounds of Callebaut chocolate from Belgium each year to make their decadent, sensual confections. There is a small bistro-style restaurant on the premises, serving waffles and pancakes for breakfast and sandwiches and wraps for lunch, but the best time to come is Saturday or Sunday brunch, when gourmet specials supplement the regular weekday fare.

SHOPPING

There's not much in the way of tourist-oriented shopping in this part of town, but if you're planning a picnic, here's where you'll find the highest concentration of natural and gourmet food stores. The largest—in fact, the

Dancing New Mexico Style

For live Norteño (traditional northern New Mexican) dance music and a local crowd, drop into **Tiny's Lounge** every Friday night. It's tucked in toward the back of a small shopping center near the intersection of St. Francis Drive and Cerrillos Road southwest of downtown. ~ 1015 Pen Road; 505-983-9817.

largest supermarket in town—is **Whole Foods Market**, offering everything from organic items in bulk to ready-made heat-and-serve meals and a wide range of deli fare. ~ 753 Cerrillos Road; 505-992-1700. There's also **Wild Oats**, which carries organic produce, healthy foods and food supplements. ~ 1090 South St. Francis Drive; 505-983-5333. **Trader Joe's** sells imported foods from around the world under its house-brand names at remarkably low prices. ~ 530 West Cordova Road; 505-995-8145.

5.

South of Santa Fe

A road tour around the area south of Santa Fe reveals New Mexico history in its unvarnished state. Whether it's the painstakingly restored Spanish Colonial ranch at las Golondrinas, the ruins of an Indian pueblo and Franciscan mission at Pecos National Monument, the ancient turquoise mines near Cerrillos or the resurrected ghost town of Madrid, the area stands apart from the 21st-century world. Exploring this wide landscape, you may feel as if you've driven into a Western movie set, and in fact many Westerns have been filmed right here.

It would be possible to visit all the sights described in this chapter in a single day, scrambling on and off Route 25 at the appropriate exits. A better plan, though, is to set your sights on just one destination—Rancho de las Golondrinas, Pecos or the twin towns of Cerrillos and Madrid—and make it the objective of a three-hour outing. In summer, plan your visit before the heat of the day sets in.

SIGHTS

About 15 miles southwest of Santa Fe is **Rancho de Las Golondrinas**, a restored Spanish hacienda dating back to 1710. It was once the last *paraje* (inn) before Santa Fe on the grueling journey along El Camino Real, the "Royal Highway," which brought traders and settlers from Mexico City to Northern New Mexico. The 200-acre grounds still operate as a working ranch, growing Indian corn and raising sheep. Coming here is like stepping back in time. Call for theme weekends. Scheduled tours run in April, May and October. Closed November through March, and

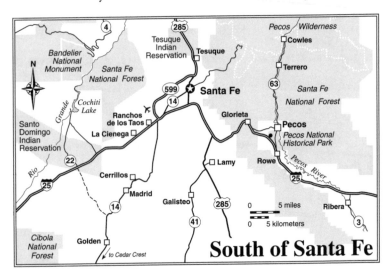

South of Santa Fe

Rancho
de las
Golondrinas

Monday and Tuesday from June through September. Admission. ~ Route 25, Exit 276, go to 334 Los Piños Road; 505-471-2261, fax 505-471-5623; www.golondrinas.org, e-mail mail@golondrinas.org.

When early pleasure travelers from the east stepped down from the Santa Fe train, they must have felt much as modern-day Amtrak passengers do when they arrive at the depot in **Lamy**, a one-street town right out of the Old West. Although Santa Fe is just over the hill, the open countryside south of the city remains mostly empty grazing land. Located 18 miles south of Santa Fe, Lamy is populated almost exclusively by artists. It's as quiet as

Lamy train depot

small towns come—except for the daily arrivals of Amtrak trains. (The station here serves Santa Fe, since the tracks there were too steep for early-day locomotives pulling full-length trains. As a result, Santa Fe–bound cars were disconnected in Lamy and pulled into the city by a shuttle.) ~ To reach Lamy by car, drive southeast (northbound) on Route 25 to exit 290. Take Route 285 south for seven miles, past the sprawling Santa Fe bedroom community of Eldorado. After you cross the railroad tracks, turn left on Route 553, which leads you into the village.

Galisteo, a tiny village about five miles south of Lamy on Route 41, dates back to the early 17th century, when a cluster of Spanish colonial haciendas appeared along the banks of the Galisteo River. In earlier centuries, the surrounding Galisteo Basin was one of the most densely populated areas in the region, with some 3000 people in 11 pueblos (one of which is currently under excavation). Perhaps it was this rich historic tradition that inspired radio personality Arthur Godfrey to build his hacienda-style home just outside of town in the 1960s. More recently, a number of New Age institutes have made their headquarters in Galisteo's larger houses. The rest of the population seems to be divided between old Spanish families and Anglo artists, many of whom keep studios here.

Route 14, known as the Turquoise Trail because American Indians have been mining turquoise in the area since ancient times, is a two-lane blacktop scenic route between Santa Fe and Albuquerque. The extension of Santa Fe's Cerrillos Road, it parallels Route 285 about ten miles to the west. To get there from Route 25, take exit 278 south; from the village of Galisteo, take unpaved County Road 42 west to Route 14.

The Turquoise Trail runs past the picturesque village of **Cerrillos**, 24 miles southwest of Santa Fe and so lost in time that filmmakers have used it as a set for Western movies such as *Young Guns*. Although in 1970 Cerrillos attained ghost town status by sinking to fewer than 100 residents, today most of the old adobes in the ten-square-block village are inhabited and a growing number of artists have established studios and galleries here. The vil-

Galisteo

Hollywood in the Hills

Since its construction in 1969 as a set for the movie *The Cheyenne Social Club*, the **J. W. Eaves Movie Ranch** has served as a location for more than 250 motion pictures, television shows and commercials. Although it is lo-

cated not far off the Turquoise Trail, it's difficult to catch a glimpse of this full-scale replica of an 1800s Western town, and it is normally not open to the public. However, when it is not in use for shooting, private tours can often be arranged directly or through your innkeeper or concierge. ~ Route 45 off Route 14; 505-474-3045.

lage church has been beautifully restored. In the rugged hills north of town, deposits of lead, turquoise and silver were mined by hand at various times, but lack of water prevented large-scale operations.

In Cerrillos, the 20-room adobe compound dubbed **Casa Grande** has been converted gradually over the years into a quaintly eccentric tourist shop, turquoise-mining museum and petting zoo. Guided four-wheeldrive tours of old Indian and Spanish turquoise diggings in the nearby hills can be arranged there. ~ Cerrillos; 505-438-3008.

The richest mineral deposit in Santa Fe County was not gold, silver or turquoise, but coal. Vast seams of both bituminous (soft) and anthracite (hard) coal honeycomb 30 square miles of mountainsides surrounding the town of **Madrid** (pronounced "MAD-rid"), three miles south of Cerrillos on Route 14. Founded in 1869, the town boomed with the arrival of the railroad in the 1880s. Within a decade, Madrid was producing 250,000 tons of coal a year and had a population larger than Albuquerque. Coal from Madrid was used to power the national nuclear laboratory in Los Alamos during World War II, but by 1954 production had ceased and the town's population had dropped to an all-time low of 13. After several years as a reputed "hideout" for motorcycle gangs, Madrid got a new lease on life in the 1980s as artists moved in and began fixing up old houses and converting abandoned company buildings into studios and galleries. Today, Madrid is the most popular destination on the Turquoise Trail both in summer and in the weeks leading up to Christmas, when the town sponsors the most spectacular lighting display in the region.

Another good daytrip destination to explore south of Santa Fe is the Pecos area. (Okay, it's *northbound* on Route 25 from Santa Fe, but this segment of the northbound interstate actually goes southeast.) After turning off the freeway at the Glorieta exit and continuing on a two-lane paved back road, you'll first pass the **Glorieta Battlefield**, the site of the westernmost skirmish of the Civil War, the 1862 Battle of Glorieta Pass. This engagement was triggered by a Texas unit of the Confederate Army that tried to capture Santa Fe as a base for the seizure of Colorado and California goldfields. Defeat of the rebels at Glorieta Pass put an end to this audacious plan.

Seven miles from Glorieta (a few miles off of Route 25 midway between the capital and Las Vegas) is **Pecos** (population 1500), a tiny town that consists of a gas station, a general store, a National Forest Service ranger station and two places typical of every New Mexican village: a Catholic mission church and a bar. Much of the pre-

Text continued on page 156.

Main Street, Madrid

Madrid has no sidewalks. The clay shoulders of the town's Main Street, also known as the Turquoise Trail, run past mining company buildings and modest frontier Victorian houses, many of them spruced up with wild color schemes and converted into artists' work-live studios. Formerly a ghost town, Madrid has risen again as the Santa Fe area's most outgoing small-town arts community—a handcrafted mix of picturesque nostalgia and cockeyed optimism.

Parking can be a problem on any summer afternoon. The most centrally located parking lot is just below the biggest building in town, the **Old Madrid Boarding House**. Today, the boarding house is a grocery market with a typical convenience store selection scattered among half a dozen parlor rooms. ~ 2885 Route 14; 505-471-5134. Nearby, the **Crystal Dragon** sells original designer jewelry as well as crystals, gemstones and rock specimens. ~ 2891 Route 14; 505-471-8888.

Walking uphill, take a look into **Seppanen & Daughters Fine Textiles**, where the wares include traditional and contemporary handmade rugs from the high plateau of Nagchuka, Tibet, as well as Navajo and Oaxacan weavings. ~ 2879 Route 14; 505-473-1963. A little farther up the street, **Java Junction Coffee & Gifts** not only serves espresso, cappuccino and baked goods but also operates the only bed and breakfast in town (see Lodging). ~ 2856 Route 14; 505-438-2772.

Gifted Hands features local and area artists. It's a hodgepodge of traditional American Indian jewelry, wall art, wearable art, Zuni fetishes, pottery and sculptures. ~ 2851 Route 14; 505-471-5943.

At the center of town you'll find a cluster of classic tourist attractions, all under the same ownership. The **Old Coal Mine Museum** contains memorabilia and detritus from 85 years of mining-town history, including a steam

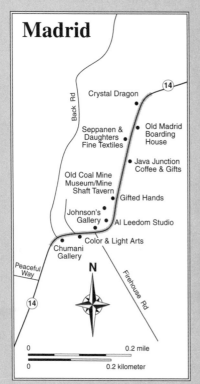

Madrid

Crystal Dragon

Back Rd

(14)

Seppanen & Daughters Fine Textiles

Old Madrid Boarding House

Java Junction Coffee & Gifts

Old Coal Mine Museum/Mine Shaft Tavern

Gifted Hands

Johnson's Gallery

Al Leedom Studio

Color & Light Arts

Chumani Gallery

Peaceful Way

(14)

N

Firehouse Rd

0   0.2 mile

0   0.2 kilometer

locomotive, antique cars and trucks, medical equipment, movie projectors and, of course, a mine shaft. Adjacent are the picturesque **Mine Shaft Tavern** (see Dining and Nightlife) and the old enginehouse that serves as the theater for the **Madrid Melodrama** (see Nightlife). ~ 2846 Route 14; 505-438-3780.

Nearby, old brick garages that were originally built to store mining equipment and vehicles have now been subdivided into a dozen or so small studio

spaces where enterprising artists come and go. Pause to look at the hillsides up above, where heaps of mine tailings spill forth, marking the places where coal was once produced in such abundance that it made Madrid the energy capital of New Mexico.

Up the hill and across the street from the Mine Shaft Tavern, **Johnson's Gallery** was the first art gallery in Madrid and is now the largest, exhibiting painting and sculpture by local artists. ~ 2843 Route 14; 505-471-1054. Adjoining Johnson's Gallery, the **Al Leedom Studio** specializes in hand-blown glass and *really* expensive, high-quality jewelry. Call ahead for a schedule of glass-blowing demonstrations. ~ 2845 Route 14; 505-473-2054.

Color & Light Arts is a small gallery that celebrates the magic of love with bright abstract paintings and prints, gleaming pottery and jewelry. ~ 2842 Route 14; 505-424-7877.

Farthest up the road is **Chumani Gallery**, the studio-gallery of contemporary painter Todd Klippenstein, who also exhibits jewelry, photography, pottery and wood carvings by other local artists. ~ 2839 Route 14; 505-424-3813.

As you reach the south end of Madrid, where old miners' shacks stand in states of hopeless disrepair and the road begins its climb over the jagged Ortiz Mountains, turn back and take your time wandering back down the hill to your car.

dominantly Spanish-speaking population ekes out a living in the surrounding national forest, cutting *vigas*, *latillas* and firewood or grazing small herds of cattle, horses and goats. Unpaved roads (many of them passable by passenger car—check at the ranger station for suggestions) lead into the forest in all directions from the village; it's a beautiful area, full of spotted, rolling hills.

When the late actress Greer Garson and her husband donated 365 acres to preserve a postclassic pueblo civilization, they made possible the creation of **Pecos National Historical Park**. Walk among ruins dating back to A.D. 1200, the remains of a pueblo thought to have stood four to five stories back in 1451 when it had a population of 2000 (more than the Pecos area today). By the 17th century the Franciscan monks had taken over the pueblo and built a pair of mission churches. You can still see the remains of the huge church, *convento* and garden walls alongside the ancient pueblo ruins. Rampant disease and famine coupled with Comanche Indian raids in the mid-1800s led to the pueblo's abandonment, but survivors moved to Jemez Pueblo, where even today they form a separate clan and speak a dialect distinct from other Indians at the pueblo. When visiting, be careful to respect the spirits that may haunt this incredible site. The ancient pueblo people were quite leery of strangers, forbidding them to set foot on pueblo land even when Pecos Pueblo was a center for trade with the Plains people. Trading parties actually had to camp outside the city wall. Admission. ~ Route 63, two miles south of Pecos; 505-757-6414 ext. 240, fax 505-757-8460; www.nps.gov/peco, e-mail peco_visitor_information@nps.gov.

Going west from the park and Pecos village, the road winds along a scenic river canyon painted with scrub oak. Along the way you'll pass a lake where the locals fish for dinner, a trout hatchery, a monastery and clusters of summer cabins. The upper Pecos River is renowned for its catch-and-release flyfishing, and on summer weekends you'll find the riverbanks lined with fishermen.

North of Pecos on Route 63 is the settlement of **Terrero**, the site of a long-abandoned refinery that used to process gold and other ores from the surrounding mountains. The pavement ends about four miles north of

HIDDEN

Hacienda Doña Andrea de Santa Fe

Six miles into the Ortiz Mountains from the village of Cerrillos on unpaved roads you'll find the **Hacienda Doña Andrea de Santa Fe**. This off-the-beaten-path bed and breakfast has spectacular views and nine

individually decorated rooms with fireplaces, shared or private patios, and an abundance of Santa Fe style. There are hiking trails on 64 private acres, and mountain bike and walking tours are available. A full breakfast and continental dinner are included in the rate. ~ 78 Vista del Oro, Cerrillos; 505-424-8995; www.hdasantafe.com, e-mail info@hdasantafe.com. ULTRA-DELUXE.

Terrero, and the unpaved road, steep and rough in spots, continues to a series of trailheads and large, well-developed campgrounds at the south portal of the Pecos Wilderness.

LODGING

Inn at Sunrise Springs
242 Los Pinos Road, La Cienega
505-471-3600, 800-955-0028, fax 505-471-7365
www.sunrisesprings.com, e-mail ellis@sunrisesprings.com
58 rooms
ULTRA-DELUXE

The Inn at Sunrise Springs, the retreat center near Rancho de las Golondrinas, features 20 spacious *casitas* with fireplaces, kitchenettes and zen studios, as well as private patios. There are also 38 hotel-style guest rooms and suites. Spring-fed pools and mature stands of cottonwoods dot the peaceful property, and there are outdoor hot tubs and a sweat lodge for guests, as well as Japanese tea ceremonies, pottery-making classes and a number of other ongoing classes.

Galisteo Inn
9 La Vega, Galisteo
505-466-8200, fax 505-466-4008
www.galisteoinn.com, e-mail reservations@galisteoinn.com
11 rooms
MODERATE TO ULTRA-DELUXE

For many weary travelers, the highlight of Galisteo is the Galisteo Inn, an authentic hacienda set on eight acres of landscaped grounds in the middle of the village. Many of the original features have been preserved, including hand-hewn *vigas*, plank floors, and antique Mexican tilework. Rooms range from a tiny twin-bedded unit to accommodations with private fireplace. Continental breakfast included.

Galisteo Inn

Java Junction

2855 Route 14, Madrid
505-438-2772, 877-308-8884
1 room
BUDGET TO MODERATE

On the other end of the price spectrum along the Turquoise Trail, Java Junction is the only B&B in Madrid— a restored miner's home (circa 1916) with a single one-bedroom suite above a coffee shop. Furnished with one queen-size bed and a rollaway bed, the air-conditioned suite features a full kitchen, a private patio and a six-foot-long clawfoot tub. The rate includes a choice of lattes, cappuccinos and fresh-baked goods from the coffee shop.

DINING

Blue Heron

The Inn at Sunrise Springs, 242 Los Pinos Road, La Cienega
505-471-3600
DELUXE

The Blue Heron is one of Santa Fe's finest restaurants, with both indoor tables and outdoor seating in a stately cottonwood and willow bosque where real blue herons can often be seen wading in natural spring-fed pools. The food is organic and uses produce and herbs grown in the inn's gardens. The brief and rather understated menu features entrées such as *hijiki*-crusted salmon in a crispy Asian noodle nest and pan-seared duck breast in red wine cherry sauce, but nothing prepares you for the stunning presentation, which includes a fresh orchid on each plate.

La Mancha Restaurant and Bar

Galisteo Inn, 9 La Vega, Galisteo
505-466-8200, fax 505-466-4008
www.galisteoinn.com, e-mail reservations@galisteoinn.com
no dinner Monday and Tuesday; lunch on Saturday; Sunday
    brunch
MODERATE TO DELUXE

La Mancha, at The Galisteo Inn, specializes in creating innovative gourmet meals using traditional New Mexico ingredients. Executive chef Enrique Guerrero was once the personal chef to the President of Mexico, and he brings an international flair to such dishes as duck *carnitas* tostadas, grilled Colorado quail with polenta and mesquite grilled New York strip. *Buen Provecho!*

PICTURE-PERFECT
Spanish Colonial Heritage Sites

1. **Rancho de las Golondrinas,** *p. 148*
2. **Pecos National Historical Park,** *p. 156*
3. **Cerrillos (old Spanish mines),** *p. 151*
4. **Galisteo village,** *p. 150*

San Marcos Cafe
3877 Route 14, Cerrillos
505-471-9298
BUDGET TO MODERATE

A friendly, folksy cafe on the Turquoise Trail, the San Marcos Cafe serves a wide array of breakfasts, including great biscuits and gravy, *machaca* (Mexican shredded beef), eggs benedict and Greek hash with poached eggs on top. There are also sandwiches and quiche for lunch. Setting just the right atmosphere for this down-home place, the windows in one of the eating areas look out on vegetable gardens and the chicken coop.

Mine Shaft Tavern
2846 Route 14, Madrid
505-473-0743
BUDGET TO MODERATE

Atmosphere is everything at the Mine Shaft Tavern, which manages to maintain its former outlaw biker road-

house look even when packed to the rafters with tourists on a summer afternoon. The fare (burgers, barbecue and pizzas) is about what you'd expect.

NIGHTLIFE

There is live rock music on weekends at Madrid's **Mine Shaft Tavern**, a roadhouse that has been in operation since 1946. There is a dancefloor and the longest bar in New Mexico. Cover on weekends. ~ 2846 Route 14, Madrid; 505-473-0743.

Cheer for the hero and heroine and boo at the villain at the **Madrid Melodrama**, situated in an old enginehouse next to the Mine Shaft Tavern. The plays are authentic Victoriana, not the familiar played-for-laughs tourist melodrama, and feature titles like *The Orphan Girl of Golden* and *Brigands of the Salty Dog*. The theater looks every bit as makeshift as the places where plays were performed in Old West mining boomtowns. The audience is urged to get rowdy and throw marshmallows at the bad guys. Admission. ~ Route 14, Madrid; 505-438-3780.

PARKS

The **Cerrillos Hills Regional Park**, just north of the village of Cerrillos, has a network of strenuous loop trails that take you to small, historic mines tucked away in the rugged, juniper-clad hills. It's ideal for horseback riding, but hikers should avoid the area in the summer, when it can be very hot. The only facilities are an information kiosk and two parking areas and trailheads. ~ To get there, take the main unpaved road from the village cen-

New Mexico and the Movies

The panoramic landscapes of New Mexico have attracted filmmakers ever since 1898, when the Edison Company made its silent movie *Indian Day School* here. Since then, the region has been chosen as the shooting location for more than 400 motion pictures, including *The Missing, All the Pretty Horses, Wild Wild West, City Slickers, Young Guns, Lonesome Dove* and *Easy Rider*.

Today, the New Mexico state government is actively promoting the state as a film production capital through tax breaks and other incentives. The film studio at the College of Santa Fe, endowed by the late actress Greer Garson who lived in nearby Pecos, is a key resource for postproduction work. The state government even plans to open a new motion picture museum in Santa Fe, in the former state archives building on Guadalupe Street.

Meanwhile, a host of movie stars have chosen to make their homes in the Santa Fe and Taos region when not working. Among them are Julia Roberts, Val Kilmer, Gene Hackman, Shirley MacLaine, Carol Burnett, Marsha Mason and Jane Fonda.

ter north across the railroad tracks and follow the signs to the park.

Trails head into the 230,000-acre **Pecos Wilderness**, the heart of the vast Santa Fe National Forest, from the upper end of Pecos River Canyon Road, which runs north for 20 miles (the last six of them unpaved and rough) to a series of campgrounds and trailheads along the wilderness boundary. From Las Vegas, a paved road leads to El Porvenir, the least-used of the Pecos Wilderness portals, at the foot of Hermit's Peak. Access to the wilderness area is by foot or horseback only; no bicycles or motorized vehicles. In addition to the wilderness area, the forest encompasses 11,661-foot Elk Mountain, the subject of a seemingly endless conservation dispute between environmentalists and timber interests, and Glorieta Mesa, an uninhabited 60-mile-long, piñon-forested "island in the sky" that can be reached on an unpaved road that climbs to the mesa top from the village of Rowe, just off Route 25. Holy Ghost, Iron Gate, Jack's Creek and Cowles campgrounds, all located along the wilderness boundary at the upper end of the Pecos River Canyon, have a total of 86 campsites (no hookups). Cowles has water, but Iron Gate does not (it does have four horse corrals). Cowles has a camping fee of $6 per night; Iron Gate, $4; Holy Ghost, $8; Jack's Creek $10. El Porvenir Campground west of Las Vegas has 13 sites (no hookups); $8 per night. ~ Route 63, 20 miles north of Pecos; and on Route 65, 17 miles northwest of Las Vegas; 505-757-6121, fax 505-757-2737.

6.
Santa Fe
to Taos

The most common sidetrip Santa Fe visitors make is to Taos, a much smaller town renowned for its picturesque Indian pueblo and its colorful history as an artists' and writers' colony. Two separate routes to Taos diverge at Pojoaque. The main highway—Routes 84/285 and 68—follows the Rio Grande for much of the way and passes several Indian pueblos. The backroad route, commonly called the High Road to Taos, winds through the Sangre de Cristo foothills and provides the only link to the outside world for small, traditional Spanish villages such as Truchas, Las Trampas and Chimayo, site of the most revered Catholic shrine in the Southwest. Many motorists drive to one way to Taos on the High Road, which takes around two-and-a-half hours, and return by the main highway, which takes half as long. (If this is your plan, avoid Española, midway between Santa Fe and Taos, on weekend evenings, when slow-cruising lowriders can paralyze highway traffic.)

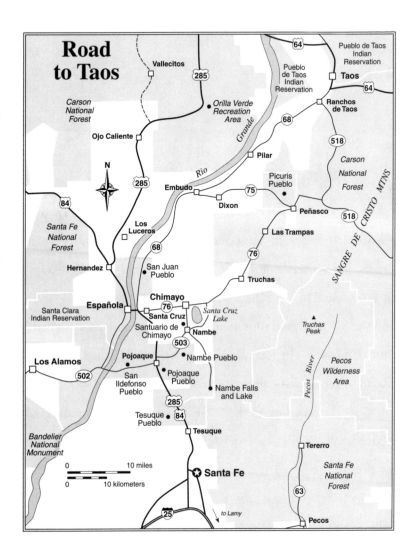

The Main Highway

The main road from Santa Fe to Taos, Routes 84 and 285 to Española and then Route 68 into the mountains to Taos, parallels the Rio Grande, where early summer motorists can see whitewater rafters and kayakers by the hundreds—and run into plenty of traffic. This route forms the main artery for sightseeing in much of northern New Mexico, including Bandelier National Monument, Los Alamos and the Tesuque, Pojoaque, San Ildefonso, Santa Clara and San Juan Indian pueblos, not to mention the gaming casinos operated by several of these pueblos.

Camel Rock

SIGHTS

The jolly sandstone Camel Rock Monolith marks the entrance road to **Tesuque Pueblo**. Considered one of the most traditional of the pueblos, Tesuque continues to have a strong agricultural emphasis, which results in organic food products for sale. Bright designs characterize their pottery. The pueblo also operates Camel Rock

Casino, where the main highway crosses tribal land. No cameras. Call for hours. ~ Route 84/285, nine miles north of Santa Fe, Tesuque; 505-983-2667, fax 505-982-2331.

Pojoaque Pueblo, one of the smallest of the northern Rio Grande Indian pueblos, hosts special fiesta days and has a visitors center where handcrafted items are sold. The pueblo's **Poeh Cultural Center** (505-455-3334) includes a museum and a reconstruction of part of the original pueblo, which was abandoned in the 1920s. The tribe has converted its old elementary school building into the glitzy neon Cities of Gold Casino. ~ Route 84/

Taking a Chance

Nothing in recent years has changed the look of New Mexico's major highways as much as the rise of Indian gaming. Advertised by glittering billboards and bright computerized displays, the state's Pueblo and Apache tribes operate 11 gambling casinos throughout the state, including four between Santa Fe and Taos. Although gaming is largely unrestricted, most casinos offer blackjack, craps, roulette, poker, Caribbean stud, pai gow poker, video poker, slot machines and bingo. Most also have budget-priced all-you-can-eat buffets.

Indian gaming has been a highly controversial topic in New Mexico since it first appeared in 1997. Opponents assert that it encourages compulsive gambling, ruins lives and drains the local economy. There can be no doubt, though, that casinos have improved the finances of Indian tribes. Visitors to Tesuque Pueblo, for instance, can see how beautifully the once-crumbling center of the pueblo has been restored, and gaming proceeds have financed the development of other businesses such as Tesuque Natural Farms, a tribal enterprise that raises llamas and grows amaranth, a traditional Aztec grain. Casinos provide employment for about 2000 people in northern New Mexico. (For specific casino information, see Nightlife.)

285, 16 miles north of Santa Fe; 505-455-3460, fax 505-455-7151 (visitors center).

Go left on Route 502 to **San Ildefonso Pueblo**, where you'll see beautiful burnished black matte pottery in the tradition of the late Maria Martinez. Current potters here continue to create artistic wonders. There's also a museum (closed weekends) on site displaying jewelry, costumes and religious artifacts. Visitors must register at the visitors center. Photography is allowed with a permit (fee). Admission. ~ Route 502; 505-455-3549, fax 505-455-7351.

From San Ildefonso, instead of returning to the main highway you can continue to Española by way of Route 30, which distantly follows the west bank of the Rio Grande across Indian lands. The main reason to take this route is to visit **Puye Cliff Dwellings**, a fascinating little ancient city. Inhabited by up to 1500 people between the years of 1250 to 1577, Puye is currently operated by the neighboring Santa Clara Pueblo, whose occupants are probably descendants of the original settlers. The excavated ruins of the ancient apartmentlike complexes are evident from miles away as you approach the site. Upon arrival, choose either the Cliff Trail or the Mesa Top Trail for exploring. Admission. The dwelling, trails and Santa Clara Canyon are all currently closed for safety reasons; call for more information. ~ Located seven miles off Route 30, south of Española; 505-753-7330.

The **Cliff Trail** takes off from above the parking lot and offers you a chance to walk through cavelike rooms and past petroglyphs and the outlines of buried masonry dwellings for more than a mile along the south face of the Puye mesa. Rock inscriptions of spirals and masks, serpents and humans are carved along the caves and cliffs. You'll also see outlines of buried masonry dwellings known as talus rooms. Stepping places and hand grips lead to kivas and the grand Community House from the cave rooms (or cavate rooms) below. Near the base of the cliffs are two kivas. But there may be more ceremonial chambers and other treasures lying undiscovered, well beneath the earth's surface.

It's possible to drive up to the second trail, appropriately called **Mesa Top Trail**, by following the road past the visitors center. From there, the Puye's 740-room pueblo, with its restored room, can be examined. Historians imagine the structure loomed as high as three stories tall. When perusing the remains, take a look around at the splendid views of the Rio Grande region. Puye villagers of so long ago likely enjoyed a similar panorama.

After exploring the cliff dwellings, drive six miles west to gorgeous **Santa Clara Canyon**, a nice place for a picnic lunch or fishing stop.

Española was founded in the 1880s as a railroad stop, although a previous short-lived settlement, originally planned as the capital of Nuevo Mexico, was founded on the site by the Spaniards as early as 1598. You'll notice the community remains true to its Hispanic heritage in everything from culture to churches. Although it has evolved into a bedroom community for Santa Fe, Española's claim to fame has always been as the "Low-rider Capital" of the world. Cruise Main Street on a Saturday night to see spiffed-up vehicles and macho young men. The heart of town—the Big Rock Shopping Center and Casino—is part of the Santa Clara Indian Pueblo; notice its namesake, an immovably big rock, in the middle of the parking lot.

Continuing north past Española, where the highway divides, drive a little farther on Route 68 to the San Juan

Pueblo sign. **San Juan Pueblo** was the site of the first capital of New Mexico in 1598. Geometric designs and luster define the red-incised pottery made here. Wood-carvings and weavings are also for sale on site. ~ 505-852-4400, fax 505-852-4820.

Near San Juan Pueblo, on the east side of the highway, stands the controversial **Don Juan Oñate Monument**. This controversial $4 million bronze statue, a larger-than-life mounted figure of the first conquistador to attempt to colonize New Mexico, is considered by some to be a political boondoggle and an affront to the Indians of the Española Valley. Latinos, however, view it as a tribute to their cultural heritage. Notice where one of Oñate's boots has been welded back on; parties unknown once sawed it off in protest because Oñate cut the left legs off Acoma Pueblo warriors following an uprising in 1608.

Continuing north on Route 68, the unpaved **River Road** parallels the highway and Río Grande. The oldest road in the valley, it serves several old haciendas that date back to colonial times. To explore it, follow any of the marked roads that turn west off the highway and intersect it. Of particular interest is **Los Luceros**, a hacienda that grew into a village and served as the county seat from 1821 to 1860.

Los Alamos and Bandelier

A detour at Pojoaque on Route 502 takes you up onto the colorful Pajarito Plateau to Los Alamos. Built during World War II on the site of a boys' ranch, this city isolated among rugged canyons was the scene of the ultimate top-secret government project—the building of the first atomic bombs. The nuclear laboratory operated by the Department of Energy is still Los Alamos' sole major employer. You can learn more about the lab's past and present activities at the **Bradbury Science Museum**, which has replicas of the first nuclear weapons ever built. ~ 15th and Central Streets, Los Alamos; 505-667-4444. Find out about the

area's geography and earliest residents, as well as Manhattan Project–era matters, at the **Los Alamos Historical Museum**. ~ 1921 Juniper Street, Los Alamos; 505-662-6272.

For a more peaceful exploration of history—and prehistory—turn south on Route 4 to **Bandelier National Monument**, where you'll find stabilized and partly restored ruins of a 12th-century Indian pueblo, cliff dwellings and a ceremonial cave along an idyllic creek in a deep canyon. The road and visitors facilities are limited to a small corner of the monument; the rest is wilderness. Ambitious hikers can try a number of rugged backcountry trails, including one to the Stone Lions, a pair of stones carved into the likeness of reclining mountain lions, which are still used ceremonially by Indians in the area. ~ Route 4; 505-672-3861.

Another 15 miles or so north on Route 68 takes you to the turnoff to the verdant town of **Dixon**, where artists hold studio visits the first weekend in November. ~ Route 75; information on studio visits: 505-579-4363.

From there it's just a couple more miles on the "river road" to Pilar and the **Orilla Verde Recreation Area**, a nice rest stop on the river's edge. (See Parks below for more information.)

If you return to Route 68 to travel north toward Taos, you'll discover that the highway was built by the U.S. Army and first called Camino Militar. Completion of this road helped end centuries' worth of isolation in Taos.

DINING

Gabriel's
Route 84/285
505-455-7000
MODERATE

A Mexican restaurant midway between Santa Fe and Pojoaque, Gabriel's serves fajitas and authentic south-of-the-border fare in a large courtyard with a colonial fountain. The chocolatey *pollo en mole poblano* is outstanding. But the restaurant's biggest claim to fame is the guacamole dip, which is mixed to order from fresh ingredients at your tableside.

Po Suwae Ge Restaurant
Route 84/285, Pojoaque
505-455-7493
MODERATE

Po Suwae Ge Restaurant in the Pojoaque Pueblo Visitors Center complex serves exclusively native pueblo foods, ranging from a piquant "three sisters stew" (corn, beans and squash) to more conventional fare such as

Indian tacos and bread pudding. The restaurant's name was the original name of the pueblo, before it was modified by the Spanish for easier pronunciation.

Anthony's at the Delta
228 Paseo de Oñate Northwest, Española
505-753-4511
dinner only
DELUXE

Anthony's at the Delta is not the kind of restaurant you'd expect to find in a working man's town like Española. For starters, the waiters wear tuxedos. The restaurant is set in a sprawling midcentury replica of a Spanish hacienda with hidden dining nooks, high beamed ceilings and old oil paintings. The food is surf-and-turf, with choices such as escargot, sea scallops, Alaskan king crab and prime rib. Reservations are essential on weekends.

Embudo Station
Route 68, Embudo
505-852-4707, fax 505-852-2479
www.embudostation.com
closed Monday and from November to mid-March
MODERATE

Mercado de las Pulgas

When you're writing a guidebook about New Mexico, it's hard to decide whether the **Tesuque Pueblo Flea Market** belongs in the shopping or sightseeing section. Just as every flea market reflects its surrounding community, this northern New Mexico gathering place contains Spanish, Anglo and American Indian traders alike. Pull over to the side of the road, shuffle through the dust and you'll find everything from pinto beans to auto parts to fine turquoise jewelry. The flea market is open every Friday, Saturday and Sunday. ~ To get there head seven miles north from Santa Fe on Route 84/285, turn left after the opera house.

Dine alfresco on the banks of the Rio Grande at Embudo Station, a glass-walled adobe restaurant located a couple miles west of Dixon and half an hour south of Taos. Green-chile beer is the novelty item on a menu of traditional favorites such as smoked trout, beef brisket and black-bean burritos.

SHOPPING

From moccasins to colorful masks and hand-coiled pottery, **Pojoaque Visitors Center** covers the gamut of American Indian folk art. It's a large gift shop, worth a good hour of browsing, and you'll no doubt walk away with a souvenir. Perhaps a storyteller doll or a kachina. ~ 96 City of Gold Road, Pojoaque; 505-455-3460, fax 505-455-7151.

NIGHTLIFE

The only nighttime action along this stretch of highway is at the several Indian casinos. The closest casino to

Santa Fe, Tesuque Pueblo's **Camel Rock Casino** is known for its Las Vegas–style showroom concerts, which run the gamut from country and Norteño bands to oldies-but-goodies rock groups. ~ Nine miles north of Santa Fe, 17486A Route 84/285, Tesuque Pueblo; 505-984-8414; www.camelrockcasino.com.

New Mexico's largest casino, **Cities of Gold** at Pojoaque operates over 700 slot machines in a building that used to be the local high school. It is also the first Indian casino in the state to build adjacent lodging accommodations. ~ Sixteen miles north of Santa Fe, 10-B Cities of Gold Road, Pojoaque; 505-455-3313; www.citiesofgold.com.

In Española, where much of the town is on Indian land, Santa Clara Pueblo's **Big Rock Casino Bowl** is located in a shopping center in the middle of town. It features 425 slot machines, as well as a restaurant and a bowling alley. ~ 419 North Riverside Drive, Española; 505-747-7625.

Meanwhile, San Juan Pueblo runs the **OhKay Casino**. ~ Route 68, one mile north of Española; 505-747-1668, 800-752-9286; www.ohkaycasino.com.

Taos Pueblo has the state's smallest gaming facility, **Taos Mountain Casino**, located near the turnoff from the highway to the pueblo. ~ Two miles north of Taos; 505-737-0777; www.taosmountaincasino.com.

PARKS

Situated on the banks of an ultrascenic stretch of the Rio Grande, **Orilla Verde Recreation Area** is renowned for its trout fishing but equally popular for hiking, biking and canoeing/kayaking adventures. The only facilities are picnic areas, showers and restrooms. Day-use fee, $3. ~

Route 570, two miles north of Pilar; 505-758-8851, fax 505-758-1620.

Camping: There are 32 campsites (no hookups); $7 per night. No water in winter.

High Road to Taos
This paved backroad route takes you through a series of traditional villages along the foothills of the Sangre de Cristo Range, where ways of life have not changed much since territorial times. Although it is only slightly longer than the main highway route—52 miles versus 45 miles—it takes about twice as long thanks to winding roads, village speed zones and irresistible photo opportunities.

SIGHTS

Drive through Pojoaque to County Road 503; turn right and drive three miles to a turnoff marked by a sign to Nambe Lake. Make a right onto the paved highway and

A Tasting Tour to Taos

Although the high desert of northern New Mexico may seem like an inauspicious place for a winery, wine grapes have been grown in the state since the 17th century. Today, New Mexico has 30 small- and medium-size wineries, including several in the valleys between Santa Fe and Taos. If you'd like to turn your drive into a wine-tasting tour, here are the places to hit. (All are open daily for tastings unless otherwise noted.)

Santa Fe Vineyards, the longest-established modern winery in the region, offers chardonnay, cabernet sauvignon and white zinfandel, as well as a house specialty called Indian Market White. ~ Route 1, Española; 505-753-8100.

Los Luceros Winery, on a historic hacienda near the Rio Grande, produces seyval blanc, vidal blanc and cayuga, as well as a special baco noir reserve aged in oak barrels. The winery building is made entirely from straw bales. Tastings on weekends only. ~ Alcalde; 505-852-1085.

Black Mesa Winery makes traditional cabernet sauvignon, merlot and zinfandel, as well as whimsically named specialty wines

wind past the cottonwoods to **Nambe Pueblo** and the sparkling Nambe Falls picnic site. This area was once a Spanish province where early settlers developed their communal land grants. Many Nambe residents are descendants of those early settlers. The falls are closed late September to mid-March. Photography fee; admission to the falls. ~ Route 1, Nambe; 505-455-2036, fax 505-455-2038.

Turn left on Route 520 and head through the Chimayo Valley to **Chimayo**. Located between the Sangre de Cristos and the Rio Grande Valley, the Chimayo Valley is a fertile area at the confluence of three streams. Within the such as Coyote, Antelope and Conejito White. The Black Beauty is a unique, chocolate-flavored red wine. ~ 1502 Route 68, Velarde; 800-852-6372.

La Chiripada Winery has been in business since 1981 and produces barrel-fermented white wines and high-quality reds as well as fruity picnic wines. ~ Route 75, Dixon; 505-579-4437.

Vivác Winery gives new meaning to the term "boutique winery." Besides its merlot and other fine wines, their tasting room also sells chocolates and fine art. ~ 2075 Route 68, Dixon; 505-579-4441; www.vivac winery.com.

Balagna Winery, the most unusual of the bunch, was established by a retired nuclear scientist from Los Alamos. In addition to its chardonnay, riesling and zinfandel, it offers specialty blends including La Bomba Grande—an irresistible souvenir with a label depicting an atomic mushroom cloud. ~ 223 Rio Bravo Drive, White Rock; 505-672-3678.

village of Chimayo is the **Santuario de Chimayo**, a place of countless miracles. Legend has it that in the early 1800s a man who saw a shining light coming from the ground dug and found a crucifix. The cross was moved to a church nearby and placed on the altar. The next morning the crucifix was gone, and found in its original location. The crucifix was moved back to the church, but again disappeared and ended up in its original location. This kept happening until people realized that someone or something wanted it to remain at this site. So, a church was built in Chimayo between 1814 and 1816. This is

Santuario de Chimayo

probably one of the reasons why people believe the Santuario's dirt is blessed. El Santuario, "The Shrine," remains a magic place where people with ailments come to experience God's healing touch. There's an annual pilgrimage to the church beginning on Good Friday. Testaments to its healing powers are everywhere, as discarded crutches, braces and *retablos* (paintings of saints done on wood) fill the church's side rooms. ~ County Road 98; 505-351-4889.

After visiting Chimayo, head north on Route 76 to the town of **Truchas** with its little weaving and wood-cutting shops. It is a burgeoning arts center whose people are undoubtedly inspired by the splendid scenery of the Sangre de Cristos and New Mexico's second-highest mountain, 13,102-foot Truchas Peak.

Continue north on Route 76 to **Las Trampas**. Once a walled adobe village—to protect it from "wild" Indians—Las Trampas is home to the 18th-century **Church of San Jose**, an oft-photographed mission church with mud plastering and early paintings. ～ Route 76, Las Trampas.

From Picuris, rejoin Route 75 for a few miles until you connect with Route 518 and pass over the landmark U.S. Hill Vista, an early, tortuous trading route. After driving over hill and dale, when Route 518 meets with Route 68, head straight to **Ranchos de Taos**. There you'll find the **Iglesia de San Francisco de Asis**, a Spanish Colonial adobe church that was the favorite of photographers like Eliot Porter and Ansel Adams. It's home to Henri Ault's amazing *The Shadow of the Cross*, which some say is miraculous. Ault's painting depicts Christ carrying a cross when observed from one angle. In different lighting, however, the cross cannot be seen. Closed Sunday. Admission to *The Shadow of the Cross*. ～ Route 68, Ranchos de Taos; 505-758-2754, fax 505-751-3923.

Those Who Paint

After passing through Las Trampas you'll come to Peñasco. Turn on Route 75 through the **Picuris Pueblo** to see the native pottery, weaving, silversmithing, beadwork and remains of a pueblo from the 13th century. Picuris, with its standing roundhouse, remains one of New Mexico's smallest pueblos. Admission. ～ Route 75, Peñasco; 505-587-2519, fax 505-587-1071.

LODGING

Casa Escondida

P.O. Box 142, Chimayo, NM 87522
505-351-4805, fax 505-351-2575
www.casaescondida.com, e-mail info@casaescondida.com
8 rooms
MODERATE TO DELUXE

Rooms at Casa Escondida are beautifully furnished with antiques and woodwork. Rooms run the gamut from a one-bedroom adobe suite to cozy single rooms with queen beds. A full hot breakfast is served in the sunny dining room. Put your feet up while lounging under their charming covered porch or slip into their outdoor hot tub. Things are quiet and peaceful here—there are no televisions at the inn.

*Iglesia de
San Francisco
de Asis*

Hacienda Rancho de Chimayo

County Road 98, Chimayo
phone/fax 505-351-2222, 888-270-2320
www.ranchodechimayo.com, e-mail rdc@espanola-nm.com
7 rooms
MODERATE

Located on the famed high road to Taos, Hacienda Rancho de Chimayo is a splendid retreat. Antique beds made of mahogany and iron, as well as traditional Chimayo handwoven draperies and rugs, give the guest rooms a homey feel. All accommodations adjoin a beautiful courtyard and have fireplaces crafted from adobe as well as pine floors and *vigas*. The inn itself is adjacent to a popular New Mexican restaurant. A continental breakfast is included in the price. This place is a real gem.

DINING

Restaurante Rancho de Chimayo

County Road 98, Chimayo
505-351-4444
www.ranchodechimayo.com
closed Monday from November through April
MODERATE

Tucked into the mountains about 40 minutes north of Santa Fe, Restaurante Rancho de Chimayo serves authentic New Mexican meals in an adobe house. The bill of fare includes tamales, enchiladas, tacos and flautas plus specialties like steak, trout, marinated pork cutlets served in a red-chile sauce and chicken breasts topped with chile sauce and melted cheese. Leave room for the homemade *sopapillas* and honey. During summer months, ask for the outdoor patio seating.

SHOPPING

For eight generations the Ortega family has been weaving brilliant sashes, vests, purses and jackets as well as world-famous rugs at their wonderful little shop, **Ortega's Weaving**. Closed Sunday. ~ At the corner of County Road 98 and State Road 76, Chimayo; 505-351-4215.

Next door, the **Galeria Ortega** is a good place to check for Southwestern gifts (pottery, kachinas, paintings, candles) and books on regional topics. Closed Sunday. ~ County Road 98 and Route 76, Chimayo; 505-351-2288.

Nambe Falls

For a sampling of local talent in Truchas, stop by the **Hand Artes Gallery**, featuring folk and fine art. Closed Sunday. ~ Route 76, Truchas; 505-689-2443, 800-689-2441; www.collectorsguide.com/handartes.

Also in Truchas is the **Cardona-Hine Gallery**, featuring the contemporary paintings of Alvaro Cardona-Hine and Barbara McCauley. ~ Off Route 76, on County Road 75, Truchas; 505-689-2253, 866-692-5070, fax 505-689-2903; www.cardonahinegallery.com.

PARKS

Nambe Falls, a double-drop waterfall tumbles down from **Nambe Lake** to a small picnic and camping area among the cottonwoods that line the Río Nambe. The lake is generously stocked with trout, and since it is on tribal land owned by Nambe Pueblo, a New Mexico fishing license is not required. Instead, anglers pay a daily fee to the pueblo; these fees are the primary source of income for this small tribe. The falls are closed October to mid-March. Day-use fee, $10. ~ To get there, turn east at Pojoaque onto Route 503 and continue for six miles, past the pueblo turnoff, to the lake entrance.

Camping: The Nambe Falls campground has 7 shelter rentals and 25 tent/RV sites with water and hookups; $20 to $30 per night. 505-455-2036, fax 505-455-2038.

7.
Taos & the Enchanted Circle

Painters Ernest Blumenschein and Bert Phillips were on their way to Mexico in 1898 when their wagon broke an axle and they found themselves stranded in Taos. Here, in the people, the landscape and the crisp mountain light, they found subject matter so compelling that their paintings inspired a generation of artists from the East and Europe to follow in their talented footsteps.

The Sangre de Cristo Mountains ("Blood of Christ") abut the town of Taos, which sits at an altitude of nearly 8000 feet on the east side; the Rio Grande River forms the city's western boundary. The Enchanted Circle is the name commonly given to an 80-mile loop route from Taos that crosses the crest of the Sangre de Cristos and circles all four sides of Wheeler Peak (elevation 13,161 feet), the highest mountain in New Mexico. The drive along the Enchanted Circle affords incomparable vistas of the heart of the high country, perspectives that could hardly help but inspire great works of art.

By the 1920s, Taos enjoyed a reputation as one of the greatest artists' colonies in America, thanks in large part to the sponsorship of local grand dame Mabel Dodge Luhan, a flamboyant New York heiress who married a man from Taos Pueblo and invited guests such as D. H. Lawrence, Georgia O'Keeffe, Ansel Adams, Willa Cather and Aldous Huxley to visit. (Her house is now a bed-and-breakfast inn.)

In the late 1960s, Taos gained brief notoriety for its hippie communes, where young urbanites attempted to return to the Pueblo Indian way of life. Clearing the land and building communal homes of adobe, they sought to create a simple lifestyle in tune with nature. Simple it wasn't. Besides the hard physical labor they experienced, these freewheeling pioneers had to cultivate their own food, debate communal politics and wrestle with the problems and possibilities of their newfound sexual freedom.

Life became a grand experiment. One of the most famous, New Buffalo Commune, was featured in *Look* and *Life* magazines, as well as *Playboy*, *Newsweek* and *Esquire*; it was also the location for an idyllic interlude in the classic '60s film *Easy Rider*. At one point, over 3000 hippies set up house in the Taos area. Although the days of drugs and free love

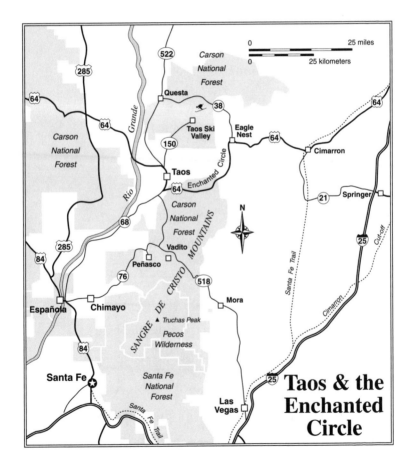

have long since vanished, the pursuit of spiritual enlightenment remains a strong force here.

But the fact that artists and idealists have taken to this part of New Mexico has hardly disrupted the deep cultural traditions that have characterized this area for thousands of years. Powwows, for instance, began in the days when Taos was one of the most distant outposts of the Rio Grande Pueblo Indians. These intertribal gatherings provided opportunities for trade, dancing and politics between the Pueblo Indians and the nomadic Arapahoe and Ute people who roamed the plains and mountains to the north. Today, powwows at Taos Pueblo attract participants from as far away as Canada. The pueblo itself draws throngs of non-Indian travelers from around the world to see this tiny, five-story town where residents continue to live without electricity or running water in accordance with ancient custom.

After the first Spanish settlers came, Taos served as a marketplace for trade between the colonists and the Indians. In the 1820s, it became an outpost where mountain men emerged from the southern Colorado Rockies to trade for supplies. (At least

one legendary frontiersman, Kit Carson, settled down in Taos, where he lived out his later years as one of the few Anglos in the Spanish and Indian community.) Today, tourism is the town's main industry. It seems that Taos residents (native Pueblo people, descendants of Spanish settlers and contemporary artists) still support themselves in the same time-honored traditions—trading with visitors from the outside world.

Taos Area   Just as Santa Fe is a unique city, Taos (population 4700) is a unique small town, not exactly easy to understand but certainly direct in its unconventionality. Painters and writers form the backbone of this peaceful yet eccentric frontier outpost, where American Indians, graying hippies and Spanish villagers co-exist peacefully. The hodgepodge of architectural styles—Victorian-era frame houses, now stuccoed over in hues of tan, clustered with adobe haciendas from the Spanish Colonial period and Indian houses stacked like honeycombs—only serves to enhance the town's compelling landscape.

Surrounded by mesas, canyons and mountain peaks, Taos has plenty of outdoor recreation year-round. The Taos Box, a wilderness canyon through which the Rio Grande tumbles and roars, offers plenty of whitewater rafting in early summer. Visitors who rent horses from the stables at Taos Pueblo can ride into the reservation's forested mountain highlands, which are otherwise off-limits to non-Indians. Hikers and backpackers find an alpine wonderland among the 13,000-foot summits of the Wheeler Peak area. For those who prefer more conventional sports, the biggest challenge to playing any of the area's golf courses and tennis courts is focusing on the ball instead of the stunning mountain scenery.

Given the superb natural setting, it's ironic that stifling gridlock and auto pollution plague Taos' main artery, Paseo del Pueblo, in all but the slowest seasons. But there's really no other way to get to Taos, and given the large local opposition to airport expansion, it could remain this way for a while. So be ecologically minded, leave your car at your residence and walk around the compact commercial core.

SIGHTS

The **Historic Taos Plaza**, as is true in so many Southwestern towns, is its lifeblood. The Plaza has remained the commercial center for tourism and throughout the centuries, three flags—Spanish, American and Mexican—have flown over the stucco buildings. Plaza galleries and shops merit at least a day's visit. You can pick up sightseeing information at the **Taos Chamber of Commerce**. Open daily in summer; closed Sunday at other times of the year. ∼ 1139 Paseo del Pueblo Sur; 505-758-3873, 800-732-8267, fax 505-758-3872; www.taoschamber. com, e-mail info@taoschamber.com.

The following five museums can be visited with one discounted ticket (available at all locations) that's both transferable and good for one year:

Blending the sophistication of European charm with a classic Taos adobe, the **E. L. Blumenschein Home and Museum** showcases the paintings of Blumenschein (a co-founder of the Taos Society of Artists); his wife, Mary Greene Blumenschein; their daughter, Helen; and many other Taos artists. The fully restored home, built in the late 1700s, is filled with furnishings from the early 20th century, as well as European antiques. Admission. ∼ 222 Ledoux Street; 505-758-0505, fax 505-758-0330; www. taoshistoricmuseums.com.

Two blocks southwest of the Plaza, at the west end of historic Ledoux Street, is the **Harwood Museum of Art**, New Mexico's second-oldest museum. A Pueblo Revival–style adobe compound, the Harwood showcases the brilliant work of the Taos Society of Artists, core of the local artists' colony. It also includes the octagonal Agnes Martin Gallery, featuring work by the internationally acclaimed artist and Taos resident. The museum's collection of 19th-century *retablos* (religious paintings on wood) will also fascinate. Closed Monday. Admission. ~ 238 Ledoux Street; 505-758-9826, fax 505-758-1475; www.harwood museum.org, e-mail harwood@unm.edu.

The **Taos Art Museum/Fechin House** is full of hand-carved woodwork in the former adobe of Russian artist Nicolai Fechin, who also designed the building. Closed Monday and Tuesday in winter, Monday in summer. Admission. ~ 227 Paseo del Pueblo Norte; 505-758-1710, fax 505-758-7320; www.taosmuseums.org.

American Indian and Hispanic art fill the **Millicent Rogers Museum**, a memorial to the late Standard Oil heiress. Within the 15 galleries are rare examples of jewelry, textiles, basketry, paintings and pottery, as well as some exhibits by contemporary artists. Closed Monday from November through March. Admission. ~ Off Route 64, four miles north of Taos Plaza; 505-758-2462, fax 505-758-5751; www.millicentrogers.org, e-mail mrm@ millicentrogers.org.

E. L. Blumen-schein Home and Museum

South of Taos at the **Martinez Hacienda**, you might discover craftsmen chinking the dark wooden walls of a sheep barn to ward off winter's cold. One of the only fully restored Spanish Colonial adobe haciendas in New Mexico, the fortresslike home is constantly being replastered to maintain its structural integrity. Inside, area artisans who perpetuate century-old skills through a living-history program demonstrate weaving, quilting, wood

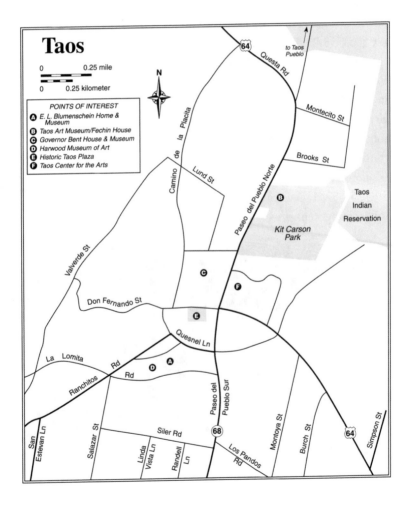

Naughty Bits

In the recesses of the La Fonda de Taos Hotel, the **D. H. Lawrence "Forbidden Art" Museum** is the smallest art museum in town. It contains 9 of the 13 naughty though rather crude paintings by the controversial author that were banned in England as obscene in 1929. The hotel bought them from the estate of Lawrence's wife, Frieda, who lived in Taos for many years after his death. Admission. ~ 108 South Plaza; 505-758-2211.

carving and other folk arts. Open daily in summer, open sporadically from November through April; call ahead. Admission. ~ Ranchitos Road, Route 240; 505-758-1000, fax 505-758-0330; www.taoshistoricmuseums.com, e-mail thm@taoshistoricmuseums.com.

Governor Bent House and Museum has American Indian artifacts and war-era memorabilia from the first governor of New Mexico. It's worth about 15 minutes of your time. Admission. ~ 117 Bent Street; 505-758-2376.

Three miles north of the city, the distant past endures at the **Taos Pueblo**, the northernmost of all pueblos. These original adobe buildings appear much as they did when Spanish explorers first viewed them in 1540. This village is a First Living World Heritage Site and follows traditional ways, with no electricity or running water for the families living in the pueblo buildings. Food is sometimes cooked in an outdoor *horno* (oven) and water is drawn from the river that breeches the heart of the pueblo. Local artisans sell mica-flecked pottery, silver jewelry,

moccasins, boots and drums here. Since the pueblo closes occasionally for ceremonial purposes, call ahead. The pueblo closes for ten weeks in late winter to early spring. Admission; camera and artist sketching fees. ~ Route 64; 505-758-1028, fax 505-758-4604; www.taospueblo. com, e-mail tourism@taospueblo.com.

Just north of the turnoff to the pueblo turn right on Route 150 for a trip to the **Taos Ski Valley**. The road rises and rolls past churches and tiny hotels through the sleepy towns of Arroyo Seco and Valdez. Making the 12-mile trip at dusk, when the light reflects from the aspen trees in ever-changing hues, can be a magical experience.

LODGING

Sagebrush Inn

1508 Paseo del Pueblo Sur
505-758-2254, 800-428-3626, fax 505-758-5077
www.sagebrushinn.com, e-mail sagebrush@newmex.com
100 rooms
MODERATE TO DELUXE

Located south of the historic district, the Sagebrush Inn looks just like any other Pueblo-style hotel from the outside. But open the hefty front door and it's a totally different world. Rooms are dark and romantic, usually decorated with Navajo rugs and pottery and equipped with fireplaces. A pool and hot tubs are nice amenities. Breakfast is included.

Casa de las Chimeneas

405 Cordoba Road
505-758-4777, 877-758-4777, fax 505-758-3976
www.visittaos.com, e-mail casa@newmex.com
8 rooms
DELUXE TO ULTRA-DELUXE

Taos bed and breakfasts are extraordinary and becoming ever more popular. Hidden on a lovely lane about

Secret Garden

On the southern outskirts of Taos, visitors can tour the **Bluebird Herb Farm**, an organic farm that grows more than 150 kinds of culinary and medicinal herbs for sale to restaurants and natural food stores throughout the Southwest. Savor the scents of rosemary, tarragon and lavender as you stroll through the large greenhouse, then wander the display gardens (children's garden, tea garden, bees and butterfly garden, potpourri garden and more). Herb teas are served after tours, and there is an herb shop on the premises. Open May through October, tour reservations required. ~ 71 Cuchilla Road, Ranchos de Taos; 505-751-1490; www.bluebirdherbfarm.com.

three blocks south of the Plaza is Casa de las Chimeneas, this guesthouse is for those who love being pampered. The largest of the rooms has a living room with a collection of books and magazines. All rooms have custom pieces by local furniture makers, tiled bathrooms and views of the formal garden and fountains. There's a hot tub on site and a large common area, as well as an exercise room, a spa, a sauna and laundry facilities. Breakfast and a buffet dinner are included in the rates.

La Posada de Taos
309 Juanita Lane
505-758-8164, 800-645-4803, fax 505-751-3294
www.laposadadetaos.com, e-mail laposada@laposadadetaos.com
6 rooms
MODERATE TO DELUXE

One of the area's original bed and breakfasts, La Posada de Taos provides a homey atmosphere in its huge

Taos Treat

Every room at **Casa Benavides Bed & Breakfast Inn** is unique, but they share a common quality—luxury. Several meticulously restored buildings, including an old trading post and an artist's studio, make up the 35-room

complex. This crème de la crème property is elegantly furnished with tile floors, handmade furniture, kiva fireplaces, down comforters and a bevy of unusual antiques. The cost of a room includes a sumptuous breakfast served in a bright, airy dining room, and afternoon tea. The inn also has lavish gardens and two hot tubs, as well as a lovely art collection. ~ 137 Kit Carson Road, Taos; 505-758-1772, 800-552-1772, fax 505-758-5738; www.taos-casabena vides.com, e-mail casabena@newmex.com. MODERATE TO ULTRA-DELUXE.

book-filled living room and open, sunny dining room. The 100-year-old house has been lovingly remodeled; each guestroom features tiled baths and antique furnishings. Five of the units are inside the inn itself, the sixth is a honeymoon cottage across the adobe-walled courtyard. All but the Taos Room sport private patios and kiva fireplaces; some have jacuzzi tubs.

La Doña Luz Inn
114 Kit Carson Road
505-758-4874, 800-758-9187, fax 505-758-4541
www.ladonaluz.com, e-mail info@ladonaluz.com
14 rooms
BUDGET TO ULTRA-DELUXE

La Doña Luz Inn is a remarkable inn. Built around a patio overflowing with flowers, each room features a spiral staircase, *vigas*, an American Indian fireplace and cowboy motifs. The whimsical Sonrisa Room has a canopied bed with a wedding-ring quilt, while the Kit Carson Room has a log bed, a sitting room with a cast-iron wood-burning stove and a clawfoot tub in the bathroom. This inn includes a wheelchair-accessible unit.

Mabel Dodge Luhan House
240 Morada Lane
505-751-9686, 800-846-2235, fax 505-737-0365
www.mabeldodgeluhan.com, e-mail
    mabel@mabeldodgeluhan.com
18 rooms
MODERATE TO ULTRA-DELUXE

Mabel Dodge, Georgia O'Keeffe, Ansel Adams, D. H. Lawrence and Dennis Hopper were but a few of the inventive minds that spent quality time at the historic, Pueblo-style Mabel Dodge Luhan House. Located on a secluded street off Kit Carson Road, its varied accommodations are charmingly decorated and offer ample opportunity to relax amid cottonwood and willow trees after a hard day of sightseeing. Reserve the glass-enclosed solarium for views of the Sacred Mountains; light up the kiva fireplace before curling up with a book on the hand-carved bed in Mabel's room. Full breakfast included.

Historic Taos Inn

125 Paseo del Pueblo Norte
505-758-2233, 800-826-7466, fax 505-758-5776
www.taosinn.com, e-mail reservations@taosinn.com
36 rooms
BUDGET TO ULTRA-DELUXE

Epicenter of Taos activity is the enormously popular Historic Taos Inn. A National Historic Landmark, the inn comprises several separate houses from the 1800s. Guest rooms are decorated in a Southwestern motif with Mexican tile, locally designed furniture and hand-loomed Indian bedspreads; most have kiva fireplaces. If the inn is booked, which it may very well be, set aside an evening to enjoy a drink in the lobby, which is as comfort-

able as any living room. A favorite hangout for locals, also known as "Taoseños."

Fechin Inn

227 Paseo del Pueblo Norte
505-751-1000, 800-811-2933, fax 505-751-7338
www.fechin-inn.com, e-mail info@fechin-inn.com

84 rooms
MODERATE TO ULTRA-DELUXE

Sharing six wooded acres with the Fechin House/Taos Art Museum, the two-story Fechin Inn is a visual wonderland that pays tribute to the Russian-born artist and long-time Taos resident, Nicolai Fechin. The eye-catching hand-carved doors, woodwork and furniture reflect his unique style within a Southwestern framework of *viga* ceilings and stucco walls. Each guest suite displays prints of his paintings; most boast fireplaces, patios or balconies. Also on the grounds are a bar, an open-air hot tub and an exercise room.

Laughing Horse Inn
729 Paseo del Pueblo Norte
505-758-8350, 800-776-0161, fax 505-751-1123
www.laughinghorseinn.com, e-mail laughinghorse@laughinghorse
    inn.com
11 rooms
BUDGET TO DELUXE

The Laughing Horse Inn is a century-old hacienda transformed into a European-style pension. As the name implies, it helps to have a sense of humor when staying here: one guest room has chile pepper–motif lights and the inn's floor varies between old wood and varnished dirt. What it may lack in luxury, it more than makes up for in personality with its low *viga* ceilings, a traditional adobe mud floor, and memorabilia from the early New Mexico literary-magazine publisher who had his printing press here. The communal kitchen offers light snacks for next-to-nothing prices. Breakfast is included.

Hacienda del Sol
109 Mabel Dodge Lane
505-758-0287, fax 505-758-5895
www.taoshaciendadelsol.com, e-mail sunhouse@newmex.com
11 rooms
MODERATE TO ULTRA-DELUXE

Certainly one of the finest bed and breakfasts in the state, Hacienda del Sol is a glorious adobe that epitomizes the Southwestern experience. Accommodations feature Spanish Colonial and American Indian decor, with twig screens and kiva fireplaces. Architectural touches include *viga* and *latilla* ceilings, stained glass and skylights. A shady stand of cottonwoods, pines, spruce and willow trees nicely blocks out nearby traffic noise. The hacienda is difficult to find, so call ahead for directions.

Dreamcatcher Bed and Breakfast

416 La Lomita Road
505-758-0613, 888-758-0613, fax 505-751-0115
www.dreambb.com, e-mail dream@taosnm.com
7 rooms
MODERATE TO DELUXE

Located in a quiet, woodsy neighborhood a short walk from Plaza, this rooms at this intimate inn are grouped around a pleasant, shaded courtyard. Choose a room with a sunken bedroom or one with traditional Southwestern furniture. Most rooms feature saltillo tile floors, kiva fireplaces, and private entrances. An outdoor hot tub is available and a full breakfast is included with a night's stay.

Salsa del Salto

Route 150, one mile north of Arroyo Seco
505-776-2422, 800-530-3097, fax 505-776-5734
www.bandbtaos.com, e-mail salsa@taosnm.com
10 rooms
MODERATE TO DELUXE

Close to the Taos Ski Area, with outrageous views of the Sangre de Cristo Mountains, is luxurious Salsa del Salto. Goose-down comforters warm the king-size beds. Leather couches in the common area are placed in front of a two-story stone fireplace—a good place for getting horizontal after a long day on Taos' tough slopes. The pool, tennis courts and hot tub help take the edge off as well. Guests rave about the omelettes served here.

Quail Ridge Inn

88 Taos Ski Valley Road
800-624-4448, fax 505-776-2949
www.quailridgeinn.com, e-mail quail@quailridgeinn.com
88 rooms
DELUXE

It's hard not to get lost while walking around the compound known as the Quail Ridge Inn. Low-slung buildings containing fully equipped apartment-size rooms dot the landscape. A casual, country-club variety of clientele clogs the pool and tennis courts. The self-contained resort offers so many on-site amenities and diversions that you need not ever leave the complex, which would be a crying shame considering all there is to see in Taos. Rates sometimes include breakfast.

Hotel St. Bernard
Taos Ski Valley Road
505-776-2251, fax 505-776-5790
www.stbernardtaos.com, e-mail stbhotel@newmex.com
28 rooms
ULTRA-DELUXE

If long days of skiing and multicourse meals are enough to satisfy you, consider a stay in the Taos Ski Valley at one of several European-flavored lodges like the simple but comfortable Hotel St. Bernard. Location, location, location and a family atmosphere prevail at this chalet-style dwelling. Reservations are usually made by the week only; all meals, lift tickets and ski school are included in the price. Closed early April through Thanksgiving.

Austing Haus B&B
Taos Ski Valley Road
505-776-2649, 800-748-2932, fax 505-776-8751
24 rooms
www.austinghaus.com, e-mail austing@newmex.com
closed mid-April to mid-May
DELUXE

Located about one and a half miles from the ski area is the Austing Haus B&B, the largest timber-frame building in North America. As the name implies, this charming bed and breakfast has an Austrian ambience. The glass dining room (open in winter only) is truly elegant.

DINING

Joseph's Table
108 South Plaza, Ranchos de Taos
505-751-4512
www.josephstable.com
no lunch on weekends
DELUXE TO ULTRA-DELUXE

Fine dining is one of my passions, and in my subjective opinion the finest in Taos is at Joseph's Table. Candlelight and frescoed walls set the stage for outstanding cuisine at this chef-owned restaurant. The menu, which changes daily, emphasizes organic ingredients. A typical dinner might be an appetizer of New Mexico squash blossoms stuffed with crab and buffalo mozzarella, followed by an entrée of apricot rosemary–glazed salmon.

Lambert's of Taos
309 Paseo del Pueblo Sur
505-758-1009
www.lambertsoftaos.com
dinner only
DELUXE TO ULTRA-DELUXE

Lamb entrées top the list of house specialties at Lambert's of Taos. Established in 1989 by the former chef at Doc Martin's, Lambert's serves imaginative presentations of mahimahi, salmon, swordfish and other fresh seafood in the parlor rooms of a refurbished Territorial-era house that exudes an atmosphere of gracious frontier living. The menu also includes beef, wild game and poultry selections.

Guadalajara Grill
1384 Paseo de Pueblo Sur
505-751-0063
BUDGET

For basic, traditional Mexican fare that's wildly popular with the locals, stop by Guadalajara Grill. Burritos, tacos and seafood plates number among many other dishes from the to-go counter at this fast food–style restaurant.

Doc Martin's
125 Paseo del Pueblo Norte
505-758-1977, fax 505-758-5776
www.taosinn.com
Sunday brunch
DELUXE TO ULTRA-DELUXE

You could eat three meals a day in the award-winning Doc Martin's and never get bored. Blue-corn and blueberry hotcakes at breakfast make the mouth water, as does seafood-stuffed tomato cannelloni for lunch. But it's at dinnertime when the kitchen really shines. Savor the grilled pork tenderloin with foie gras butter and specials like the piñon-crusted salmon with pesto and try to save room for dessert.

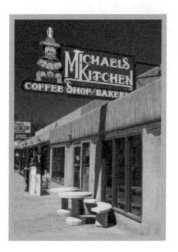

Michael's Kitchen
304 Paseo del Pueblo Norte
505-758-4178
www.michaelskitchen.com, e-mail ninne
man@michaelskitchen.com
closed in November
MODERATE

The funky sign on local institution Michael's Kitchen might grab you, but the sweets' cabinet could lock you into a stranglehold. Spill-off-your-plate-size breakfasts pack 'em in on ski mornings; diner-type meals are served the rest of the day.

Meatless on Main Street

Delicious whole-grain breads and fresh-squeezed juices (plus tarts to undo all the good you've put in your body) are common at the **Main Street Bakery**, which specializes in vegetarian and vegan fare. If you're shy about garlic, don't order the home-style potatoes. This is a great place to catch up on local gossip. Breakfast and lunch weekdays, breakfast until 12 p.m. on weekends. ~ 112 Doña Luz Road, Taos; 505-758-9610. BUDGET.

Apple Tree
123 Bent Street
505-758-1900
e-mail appletree@newmex.com
Sunday brunch
MODERATE TO ULTRA-DELUXE

The emphasis is on fresh ingredients at the Apple Tree, a charming house converted into a restaurant. The Apple Tree offers innovative interpretations of standard poultry, fish and meat dishes. Killer desserts top off the menu.

Ogelvie's
103-1 East Plaza
505-758-8866, fax 505-758-0728
MODERATE

With the best view in town of the central plaza from its second-story balcony, Ogelvie's serves such Southwest Nouveau cuisine as trout piñon and garlic and pepper ribeye steaks. Traditional New Mexican dishes such as quesadillas and chicken or beef fajitas are also served in this dimly lit restaurant and lounge.

Momentitos de la Vida Restaurant
474 Route 150, Arroyo Seco
505-776-3333
www.vidarest.com, e-mail vida@newmex.com
dinner only
MODERATE TO ULTRA-DELUXE

The New American cuisine featured here is prepared with fresh, organic ingredients whenever possible. Menu recommendations (and it's all recommended) include the soft-shell crab and prawn tempura appetizer, the wild Russian boar tenderloin, and the lobster risotto. You'll be sure to find the perfect accompaniment from their extensive wine list. There's also a casual bistro with moderately priced fare on the premises.

Tim's Stray Dog Cantina
Cottam's Alpine Village, Taos Ski Area
505-776-2894, fax 505-776-1350
e-mail straydog@newmex.com
BUDGET TO MODERATE

Sate après-ski hunger by moseying on down the hill to Tim's Stray Dog Cantina. Quaff multiple varieties of margaritas served in pitchers while chowing down on the *piri-piri* shrimp, homemade green-chile stew and mud pie that will push your cholesterol count right off the Richter scale.

SHOPPING

The Taos "mystique" has always lured artists and craftsmen, so expect to find lots of shops and galleries around the Plaza and surrounding streets.

For a deal on moccasins, stop by the **Taos Moccasin Company.** ~ 216 Paseo del Pueblo Sur; 505-751-0032; www.taosmocs.com. **Old Taos Traders** is a traditional favorite for Mexican imports. ~ 127 North Plaza, Taos; 505-758-1133.

Antiques and beautiful oriental rugs fill the front and back yards of **Patrick Dunbar Colonial Antiques**, which is interesting to visit even if you can't afford a single thing. Closed Sunday in winter. ~ 222 Paseo del Pueblo Norte, Taos; 505-758-2511.

Touristy, yes, but wonderful too, is R. C. Gorman's **Navajo Gallery**, which specializes in Gorman's paintings and sculpture of Navajo women. ~ 210 Ledoux Street, Taos; 505-758-3250; www.rcgormangallery.com.

Taos has a plethora of art galleries. Here's a sampling of what you'll find. **The Clay and Fiber Gallery** has beautiful bowls, jewelry and textiles. Closed Sunday in winter. ~ 201 Paseo del Pueblo Sur; 505-758-8093. The **New Directions Gallery** specializes in contemporary Taos painting and sculpture. ~ 107 North Plaza, Suite B; 505-758-2771; www.newdirectionsgallery.com. **Taos Artisans Gallery** is an impressive cooperative showcasing iron sculpture, jewelry, pottery and woven clothing. ~ 107-A Bent Street; 505-758-1558. Another gem of an art cooperative is **Open Space Gallery**, where more than a dozen local artists show their work. ~ 103-B East Plaza, Taos; 505-758-1217.

There are many great bookstores in Taos. A favorite is **Moby Dickens Bookshop**, which has plenty of places to sit and read. A cat named Ruby guards the door. ~ 124-A Bent Street; 505-758-3050. **Brodsky Bookshop** has lots of new and used American Indian and Southwestern titles as well as poetry and literature. Closed Sunday. ~ 226-A Paseo del Pueblo Norte; 505-758-9468.

La Lana Wools uses fine natural fibers to make sweaters, coats, yarns and jackets. Native plants are used to dye the fiber. ~ 136 Paseo del Pueblo Norte, Taos; 505-758-9631; www.lalanawools.com. **Taos Mountain Outfitters** sells outdoor garb and equipment for trekking into the high country. ~ 114 South Plaza, Taos; 505-758-9292; www.taosmountainoutfitters.com.

NIGHTLIFE

For a taste of local flavor, swing by the **Taos Inn's Adobe Bar**. Jazz, flamenco and American Indian flute can be enjoyed several nights a week. ~ 125 Paseo del Pueblo Norte, Taos; 505-758-2233; www.taosinn.com.

The **Taos Center for the Arts** hosts a variety of events ranging from films and music and dance performances to art shows that suit all tastes and ages. ~ 133 Paseo del Pueblo Norte, Taos; 505-758-2052; www.taoscenterforthearts.org.

You'll find plenty of Western-style dirty dancing at the **Sagebrush Inn Bar**, which features live music and country-and-western dancing. No music Sunday through Wednesday. ~ 1508 Paseo del Pueblo Sur, Taos; 505-758-2254.

Taos' best sports bar, complete with brewpub and a boisterous crowd, is the **Old Blinking Light**, which occasionally features live music. Don't leave without trying a margarita. ~ Mile Marker 1, Ski Valley Road, Taos; 505-776-8787.

PICTURE-PERFECT
Local Hangouts

1. **Doc Martin's,** *p. 206*
2. **Ogelvie's,** *p. 207*
3. **Old Blinking Light,** *p. 210*
4. **Tim's Stray Dog Cantina,**
   p. 208, 211

For a drink in the Taos Ski Valley, check out the margaritas at **Tim's Stray Dog Cantina.** ~ 105 Sutton Place, Taos Ski Area; 505-776-2894. Just 150 yards from the main lift at the Taos Ski Area, the Thunderbird Lodge's **Twining Tavern** is another good bet. Closed mid-April to mid-December. ~ 3 Thunderbird Road; 505-776-2280.

PARKS

Kit Carson Park is a 25-acre verdant park in the center of town that houses the grave of frontiersman Kit Carson. There are picnic areas, a playground and restrooms. ~ 211 Paseo del Pueblo Norte, Taos; 505-758-8234, fax 505-758-2493; www.taosgov.com, e-mail dmartinez@ taosgov.com.

The challenge of scaling Wheeler Peak, whose 13,161-foot summit is the highest point in New Mexico, brings mountaineers from all over the country to **Carson National Forest.** The lower, gentler mountains southeast of Taos, which local villagers have been using communally as a source of firewood and summer pasturage for centuries, contain hundreds of miles of rough forest roads, many of which are ideal for hiking, mountain-bike and four-wheel-drive adventures in the summer months and cross-country skiing in the winter season. Some say that the fishing here is the best in the state: rainbow, brown and native Rio Grande cutthroat trout inhabit the park's many lakes and cold water streams. Farther south, the 13,102-foot Truchas Peak crowns the roadless immensity of the Pecos Wilderness. Roads and amenities are closed January through April. ~ Accessed by Route 150 (Taos Ski Valley Road) and by Routes 518, 75 and 76 (collectively called the High Road to Taos); 505-758-6200, fax 505-758-6213; www.fs.fed.us/r3/carson.

Camping: Capulin and La Sombra Campgrounds, one half mile apart on Route 64 about seven miles east of Taos, have a total of 24 tent/RV sites (no hookups); $8 to $15 per night. Farther west, off of Route 518 near Tres Ritos, Agua Piedra and Duran Canyon Campgrounds have a total of 56 sites (no hookups); $8 to $15 per night. These campgrounds are closed October through April.

Enchanted Circle Area

The Enchanted Circle is the name given to the 84-mile loop formed by Routes 522, 38 and 64. From Taos, the paved route winds through subalpine evergreen forests around the base of Wheeler Peak, the highest mountain in New Mexico (elevation 13,161 feet). Along the way you'll find ski resorts, a recreational lake in a basin surrounded by mountain peaks, and a moving tribute to the men and women who served in the Vietnam War.

SIGHTS

Drive south of downtown Taos to Route 64 and cruise over scenic **Palo Flechado Pass**, which was used by American Indians and Spaniards who came from the plains via the Cimarron River. Along the way are several places to pull over for a picnic or snapshot.

Upon reaching the intersection of Route 434, turn south for a quick visit to the resort town of **Angel Fire**. In winter it's a favorite destination for intermediate skiers, while in summer, golfers, hikers and lovers of chamber music flock to Angel Fire.

Back on Route 64 you'll soon come to **Eagle Nest Reservoir**, a fine sailing, windsurfing and fishing lake that affords a spectacular lookout. Be sure to get a good look at **Wheeler Peak**, the state's highest peak at 13,161 feet above sea level. On a hillside overlooking Eagle Nest Reservoir, the **Vietnam Veterans National Memorial** pays tribute to soldiers who fought in Vietnam. Set against the backdrop of the Sangre de Cristo Mountains, this 24-acre monument is one of the largest in the country. It includes a visitors center with extensive exhibits dedicated to the memory of those who lost their lives as well as access to computerized archives of KIA (killed in action) and MIA (missing in action) soldiers. There's an

Vietnam Veterans National Memorial

interdenominational chapel on the premises. ~ Route 64, Angel Fire; 505-377-6900, fax 505-377-3223; www.angel firememorial.com, e-mail memorial@taosnet.com.

At the lake's north shore is the village of **Eagle Nest**, with a handful of restaurants and shops. From there it's 24 windy miles to Cimarron through the Cimarron Range (one of the easternmost ranges of the Sangre de Cristo Mountains), the Colin Neblett Wildlife Area and Cimarron Canyon. Three miles east of Eagle Nest are the towering walls of **Cimarron Canyon State Park**. Be sure to watch your speed, and after dark be on the lookout for deer as you travel through the narrow canyon. ~ Route 64; 505-377-6271.

Return to Eagle Nest; just north of the town (where Route 64 becomes Route 38) is an open and pretty valley ringed with high mountains. Drop down Bobcat Pass

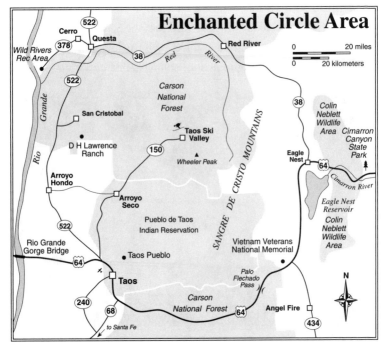

Ghostly Walls

Midway between Angel Fire and Eagle's Nest on the Enchanted Circle route lies **Elizabethtown**, once a boomtown with a population of 7000 (larger than present-day Taos). It was the population center of the Moreno Valley mining district, which yielded $5 million worth of gold ore. The town was abandoned in the 1920s after the mines closed. Today, the site is marked by the stone ruins of the old Mutz Hotel, foundations of a general store and other buildings. Area residents have established a small museum just up the road, open in summer. ~ West side of Route 38; 505-377-3420.

into **Red River**, yet another Wild West village. Though touristy, this early-20th-century goldmining town retains a certain charm from its rip-roaring gambling, brawling and red-light district days. A ski area rises out of its center and national forest land surrounds it completely.

Continuing east on the Enchanted Circle, which hugs Red River, you'll drive past plenty of forest and camping spots until you reach the honey-producing town of **Questa**. From Questa, 22 miles south on Route 522 will bring you back to Taos.

Just 11 miles southwest of Questa, where the Enchanted Circle tour rejoins the main highway, is the **Wild Rivers Recreation Area**, the ideal place to see the Rio Grande and Red River in their natural state. The Art Zimmerman Visitors Center features geologic exhibits, interpretive displays and rangers who will help you make the most of this scenic area. Most visitors flock to La Junta Point overlooking the junction of these free-flowing rivers. Self-guiding nature trails show you how the Rio Grande Gorge was etched out over the centuries by wind and water. The numerous hiking trails in this area include several steep climbs leading down to the water. Proceed with caution. Admission. ~ Route 378; 505-770-1600, 505-758-8851, fax 505-751-1620; www.nm.blm.gov.

Thirteen miles south of Questa is the **D. H. Lawrence Ranch**, a memorial to the British writer built by his widow, Frieda. When Mabel Dodge Luhan gave the land that is now the D. H. Lawrence Ranch to the writer's wife, Frieda returned the favor with a gift: the original manuscript to *Sons and Lovers*. Now a field center for the University of New Mexico, it can be readily visited during the daytime hours. ~ Off Route 522, 20 miles north of Taos; 505-776-2245, fax 505-776-2408.

Another 13 miles south is the junction of Routes 522 and 64. Go west on Route 64 until you reach the **Rio Grande Gorge Bridge**. You may want to hold your breath while crossing this suspension bridge, 650 feet over the Rio Grande.

LODGING

Wildflower Bed & Breakfast
P.O. Box 575 (40 Halo Pines Terrace), Angel Fire, NM 87710
505-377-6869
www.angelfirenm.com/wildflower, e-mail wildflower@afweb.com
5 rooms
MODERATE TO DELUXE

The Wildflower Bed & Breakfast is a traditionally designed contemporary home with a wide front porch and sunny back deck area, both looking out on meadows that are full of colorful native flowers in the warm months. Second-floor dormers contain the guest bedrooms; three have private baths. Perhaps the best part of a stay at this B&B is the gourmet breakfast, featuring such items as banana french toast, Swedish oatmeal pancakes and sourdough biscuits with eggs. There's a two-night minimum stay in winter.

Cottonwood Lodge

124 East Therma Street, Eagle Nest
505-377-3382, 800-377-3955, fax 505-377-2446
www.angelfirenm.com/cottonwood, e-mail cottonwood@angel
   firenm.com
3 rooms
MODERATE

The guest accommodations at Cottonwood Lodge
are situated above the Enchanted Circle area's most
unique gift store (items featured are chainsaw-carved).
Each of the units opens onto a conversation area, and
each has a TV with VCR and a full kitchen with mi-
crowave and dishwasher; the rooms are furnished with
antiques. The shore of Eagle Nest Reservoir is just a short
walk away.

*mural by
George
Chacon*

DINING

The Lodge at Red River
400 East Main Street, Red River
505-754-6280, 800-915-6343
www.redrivernm.com/lodgeatrr, e-mail lodge@redrivernm.com
breakfast, lunch and dinner; closed April to mid-May and late
    October to mid-November
MODERATE TO DELUXE

Eager to trade fast-food drive-ins for a table set with real silverware? Then take a seat in the beam-ceilinged dining room at The Lodge at Red River. Specialties like rainbow trout, charbroiled pork chops and fish tacos will make up for all the cheeseburgers you've suffered. Entrées come with salad or soup and vegetables, and extra helpings on these items are available at no extra charge. The bar is a pleasant après-ski stop.

Angel's Coyotes
112 West Main Street, Red River
505-754-6177
reduced hours during the off-season; call ahead
BUDGET TO MODERATE

PICTURE-PERFECT
Spectacular Views

1. **Taos Ski Valley road,** *p. 196*
2. **Rio Grande Gorge Bridge,** *p. 216*
3. **Wheeler Peak from Eagle Nest
   Reservoir,** *p. 213*
4. **Cimarron Canyon State Park,** *p. 214*
5. **Wild Rivers Recreation Area,** *p. 215*

You can't top Angel's Coyotes for chicken-fried steak, *Red River* enchilada plates and a generous soup and salad bar. The Southwest-style pastel decor includes ceiling fans and booth seating.

NIGHTLIFE

Music from Angel Fire is a great place to rub elbows with New Mexico's patrons of the arts. Since 1983, the organization has hosted a variety of rotating artists whose music will soothe the most savage of beasts. There are also regular chamber music recitals and a festival in the summer. ~ P.O. Box 502, Angel Fire, NM 87110; 505-377-3233, 888-377-3300, fax 505-989-4773; www.music fromangelfire.org, e-mail info@musicfromangelfire.org.

Over the mountain in Red River, stop in at **Bull o' the Woods Saloon**, where a deejay plays country music and classic rock, and there's live music on weekends during the summer. Closed in April. ~ 401 Main Street;

505-754-2593. A bar with live country-and-western on weekend nights is the **Motherlode** at The Lodge at Red River. Closed April and May. Cover. ~ 400 East Main Street, Red River; 505-754-6280.

Melodramas are staged several nights a week from mid-June to mid-August at the **Red River Inn**. Call ahead for performance days and times. ~ 300 West Main Street, Red River; 505-754-2937.

PARKS

Like the Santa Fe National Forest, which adjoins it on the south, **Carson National Forest** is split by the Rio Grande Valley into two separate units, with numerous trails for hiking, biking and horseback riding throughout. The western part extends from the spectacular red, white and yellow cliffs around Abiquiu northward to the Colorado state line, encompassing the gently rolling pine forests of the San Pedro and Canjilon Mountains. The portion of the Rio Chama above Abiquiu Lake has been designated a National Wild and Scenic River by the U.S. Congress and is a popular rafting area. The Canjilon Lakes and a number of other remote lakes reached by forest roads in the north are favorites with local anglers. ~ Accessed by numerous forest roads off Route 84 between Española and Chama; 505-684-2486, fax 505-684-2486; www.fs.fed.us/r3/carson.

Camping: The lakeside campground at Canijilon Lakes has 40 sites (no hookups); $5 per night. Closed September through May.

In **Cimarron Canyon State Park**, granite formations tower above a sparkling stream where brown and rainbow trout crowd the waters and wildlife congregates. There are some trails suitable for hiking, biking and

Carson
National
Forest

horseback riding, but fishing is the most popular park activity. Facilities are limited to picnic areas and restrooms. ~ Route 64, 14 miles west of Cimarron; 505-377-6271, fax 505-377-2259.

Camping: There are 88 developed sites (no hookups); $10 per vehicle per night. No water from mid-September to early May. Reservations: 888-664-7787.

Index

Dining and Lodging Index

PHOTO CREDITS

Photographs © Ellen and Hank Barone, except those listed below:

Photographs on the following pages courtesy of the New Mexico Department of Tourism: page 19 (Dan Monaghan); page 21 (Mark Nohl); page 22 (Mark Nohl); page 29; page 32 (Mike Stauffer); page 58; page 73 (Dan Monaghan); page 81; page 88 (Dan Monaghan); page 94; page 152 (Mark Nohl); page 154; page 171

Photograph on page 157 courtesy of Hacienda Doña Andrea de Santa Fe (Anne Contreras)

Hidden Picture-Perfect Escapes Guides

More Americans than ever before live in large metropolitan areas. So when they want to get away from it all, they go to smaller, quieter, more welcoming spots that leave the traffic and other anxieties of big-city life behind. This series zeros in on just those types of charming getaway spots. By dedicating an entire book to a friendly little destination, each guide is able to offer a variety of features and a depth of coverage unmatched by more general guides.

Hidden Guides

Adventure travel or a relaxing vacation?—"Hidden" guidebooks are the only travel books in the business to provide detailed information on both. Aimed at environmentally aware travelers, our motto is "Where Vacations Meet Adventures." These books combine details on unique hotels, restaurants and sightseeing with information on camping, sports and hiking for the outdoor enthusiast.

Ulysses Press books are available at bookstores everywhere.
If any of the following titles are unavailable at your local bookstore,
ask the bookseller to order them.

You can also order books directly from Ulysses Press
P.O. Box 3440, Berkeley, CA 94703
800-377-2542 or 510-601-8301
fax: 510-601-8307
www.ulyssespress.com
e-mail: ulysses@ulyssespress.com

HIDDEN GUIDEBOOKS

____ Hidden Arizona, $16.95
____ Hidden Bahamas, $14.95
____ Hidden Baja, $14.95
____ Hidden Belize, $15.95
____ Hidden Big Island of Hawaii, $13.95
____ Hidden Boston & Cape Cod, $14.95
____ Hidden British Columbia, $18.95
____ Hidden Cancún & the Yucatán, $16.95
____ Hidden Carolinas, $17.95
____ Hidden Coast of California, $18.95
____ Hidden Colorado, $15.95
____ Hidden Disneyland, $13.95
____ Hidden Florida, $18.95
____ Hidden Florida Keys & Everglades, $13.95
____ Hidden Georgia, $16.95
____ Hidden Guatemala, $16.95
____ Hidden Hawaii, $18.95
____ Hidden Idaho, $14.95
____ Hidden Kauai, $13.95
____ Hidden Los Angeles, $14.95

____ Hidden Maui, $13.95
____ Hidden Montana, $15.95
____ Hidden New England, $18.95
____ Hidden New Mexico, $15.95
____ Hidden New Orleans, $14.95
____ Hidden Oahu, $13.95
____ Hidden Oregon, $15.95
____ Hidden Pacific Northwest, $18.95
____ Hidden Salt Lake City, $14.95
____ Hidden San Diego, $14.95
____ Hidden San Francisco & Northern California, $18.95
____ Hidden Seattle, $13.95
____ Hidden Southern California, $18.95
____ Hidden Southwest, $19.95
____ Hidden Tahiti, $17.95
____ Hidden Tennessee, $16.95
____ Hidden Utah, $16.95
____ Hidden Walt Disney World, $13.95
____ Hidden Washington, $15.95
____ Hidden Wine Country, $13.95
____ Hidden Wyoming, $15.95

HIDDEN PICTURE-PERFECT ESCAPES

____ Charleston, $14.95
____ Palm Springs, $14.95

____ Santa Barbara, $14.95

Mark the book(s) you're ordering and enter the total cost here ➡ [   ]

California residents add 8.75% sales tax here ➡ [   ]

Shipping, check box for your preferred method & enter cost here ➡ [   ]

❏ BOOK RATE   **FREE! FREE! FREE!**

❏ PRIORITY MAIL/UPS GROUND   cost of postage

❏ UPS OVERNIGHT OR 2-DAY AIR   cost of postage   [   ]

Billing, enter total amount due & check method of payment ➡

❏ CHECK   ❏ MONEY ORDER

❏ VISA/MASTERCARD_____EXP. DATE_____

NAME_____PHONE _____

ADDRESS _____

CITY_____ STATE_____ ZIP _____

MONEY-BACK GUARANTEE ON DIRECT ORDERS PLACED THROUGH ULYSSES PRESS.

ABOUT THE AUTHOR

Richard Harris has written or co-written 35 other guidebooks including Ulysses' *Hidden Miami, Hidden Baja, Hidden Belize, Hidden New Mexico, Hidden Cancún and the Yucatán, Weekend Adventure Getaways: Yosemite Tahoe* and the bestselling *Hidden Southwest*. He has also served as contributing editor on guides to Mexico, New Mexico, and other ports of call for John Muir Publications, Insight Guides, Fodor's, Birnbaum and Access guides. He is a past president of PEN New Mexico and currently president of the New Mexico Book Association. When not traveling, Richard writes and lives in Santa Fe, New Mexico.

ABOUT THE PHOTOGRAPHERS

Ellen and Hank Barone are New Mexico–based travel writers/photographers who have circled the globe on assignment for regional, national and international clients. Recent assignments have taken them to Southeast Asia, Alaska, Costa Rica, Italy, Mexico and the Caribbean. The Barones run International Media Group (www.intl mediagroup.com), which supplies stock photography and self-illustrated features to travel-industry clients.